C000071794

UK LIGHT RAIL
and Tram Museum
GUIDE 2017

Written by Nick Meskell & David Umpleby

Designed by Jason Prescott

Published by Train Crazy Publishing

© 2017 Train Crazy Publishing

All rights reserved. No part of this book may be reproduced or transmitted in any form
or by any means, electronic or mechanical, including photocopying, scanning,
recording or by any information storage and retrieval system, without written
permission from the publisher.
Published by:
Train Crazy Publishing, Videoscene, PO Box 243, Lytham St Annes. FY8 9DE
email: sales@videoscene.co.uk

Contents

UK LIGHT RAIL
and Tram Museum
GUIDE 2017
Locations

Introduction

Primarily due to the expansion of the systems in Nottingham, Manchester and Birmingham and improved services in Blackpool, official figures from the Department for Transport show that a staggering 252 million people travelled on a modern tram or light rail vehicle in England during 2015/2016. This is an increase of 5.8% on the previous year. 21 million vehicle miles were operated, £337m was paid in fares and there are now 397 stations/stops and a total of 494 carriages!

Welcome to our 2017 guide. As usual this edition is crammed full of information and images and with a new format, all fully updated, we hope you enjoy the book.

You'll notice straight away that we've stuck with the larger A5 size this year. We've included the Docklands Light Railway and the Tyne and Wear Metro again; although not trams as such, they still come under the light rail banner. The book is split into six chapters featuring 30 systems and/or museums and as it was so well received last year, the feature on Cliff Lifts is retained!

I would like to thank all the contributors to this edition, in particular Phil Wimbush and James Millington. A massive thank you is extended to everybody who provided images, especially the individuals who contributed to the Cliff Lift section. Without your help this book wouldn't have been possible.

Nick Meskell and **David Umpleby**
March 2017

The Internet and other publications - Due to the huge current interest in UK Light Rail systems a number of similar publications have been produced, either online or in print form. During the process of compiling this edition, cross reference was made between some of these, with numerous errors discovered. This is particularly true with the internet, as it has become customary to copy information. This leads to an assumption that if a statement appears on two or three websites, it must be 'correct' although in fact the first one was wrong or out-of-date! Details of advert liveries and names carried by the trams are also often incorrect. Efforts are made to record new names and adverts when they applied but records are often not updated when they are removed. For example, it would appear that 'dozens' of Manchester trams have advert vinyls when in reality, as was observed during a visit to this system during February 2017, very few actually do! Further to this, even official information which is published online by the various systems can be incorrect.

As is the nature of a publication like this, there will be mistakes and out-dated information but the authors have made an effort to visit all of the modern light rail systems and museums during 2016/2017 and compile as much updated information as possible. Hopefully what is included here is accurate. If you do spot a mistake, please contact us so we can improve future editions.

Content - The information provided in this book has been obtained from official sources as well as our observations when visiting the systems, updated to March 2017. The fleet lists provided are updated to 10th March 2017. The list of tram and advert liveries is ever changing, particularly advertising liveries. These can last as little as a few weeks or be modified at short notice.

Maps - The maps used in this publication are our versions of the official maps published by the various operators. These are to be used only as a rough guide and connections to railway stations etc are not shown. Not all of the stops shown are open all of the day or at weekends and some do not have disabled or wheelchair access. Please use the official maps provided or check with the operator before travelling.

Copyright © Train Crazy Publishing March 2017. All rights reserved. No part of this book may be reproduced or transmitted in any form or by any means, electronic or mechanical, including photocopying, recording, scanning or by any information storage and retrieval system, on the internet or elsewhere, without permission from the publisher in writing. **Copyright:** Illegal copying and selling of publications deprives authors, publishers and retailers of income, without which there would be no investment in new publications. Unauthorised versions of publications are also likely to be inferior quality and contain incorrect information. If you are aware of this, you can help by reporting copyright infringements, theft, plagiarism and acts of piracy to the publisher or the UK Copyright Service.

Front cover: Testing of the new Class 399 tram/trains commenced in March. This is 399201 at Sheffield station. *Phil Wimbush* (Note: This replaces the original yellow cover/Manchester tram which is now on the back cover).

Back cover: 3120+3119 pick their way over the new point work at Manchester Victoria railway station in January 2017. *DU*

Light Rail Metros

Docklands Light Railway
London

Vital Statistics

Opened: 1987
Owner: TfL
Operator: KeolisAmey Docklands Ltd
Number of lines: Four
Number of stations/stops: 45
Depots: Beckton and Poplar
Route mileage: 23 (37km)
Power supply: 750V DC third rail
Track gauge: 4ft 8 1/2in (1435mm)
Website: www.dlrlondon.co.uk
Passenger journeys: 116.9 million in
  2015/16 (+6.1% on 2014/15)
Passenger revenue: £161.9 million in
  2015/16 (+12.3% on 2014/15)
Vehicle miles: 3.8 million in 2015/16
  (+3.7% on 2014/15)

35 and 72 drop down the gradient from Crossharbour to the stop at the delightfully named Mudchute. Crossharbour has a turn-back siding in the middle, which can just be made out in the distance and Mudchute has a rarely used platform on the left hand side. 35 is part of the B90 stock built in 1991-92; 72 is from the B92 stock built in 1993-95. DU

Timeline

1985: Construction began.
1987: Passenger services began on the two routes: Tower Gateway to Island Gardens and Stratford to Island Gardens.
1991: First major extension to Bank via a tunnel to the deep level tube station allowed interchange with London Underground services.
1994: A major route extension opened from Poplar to Beckton via Canning Town. Beckton depot opened.
1996: Beckton depot expanded.
1999: Extension to Lewisham opened.
2005: Extension to King George V dock opened.
2009: Extension to Woolwich Arsenal opened.
2011: In connection with the 2012 Olympic Games, a line was built between the existing stations at Canning Town and Stratford, including four new stations, running on the former North London Line. A short extension was added from Stratford to Stratford International.

Routes

The DLR has five principal operating routes: Bank to Woolwich Arsenal, Bank to Lewisham, Tower Gateway to Beckton, Stratford to Canary Wharf and Stratford International to Woolwich Arsenal.

Timetables

Bank to Woolwich Arsenal: From Bank the first trains are: 05.33 (M-F), 05.32 (Sat), 07.02 (Sun). Last trains are: 00.33 (M-F), 00.32 (Sat), 23.32 (Sun). From Woolwich Arsenal the first trains are: 05.31 (M-F), 05.31 (Sat), 07.01 (Sun). Last trains are: 00.11 (M-F), 00.11 (Sat), 23.11 (Sun). Trains run every ten minutes daily, increased to every eight minutes at peak times on weekdays.

Bank to Lewisham: From Bank the first trains are: 05.30 (M-S), 07.00 (Sun). Last trains are 00.30 (M-S), 23.30 (Sun). From Lewisham the first trains are: 05.28 (M-S), 06.59 (Sun). Last trains are:

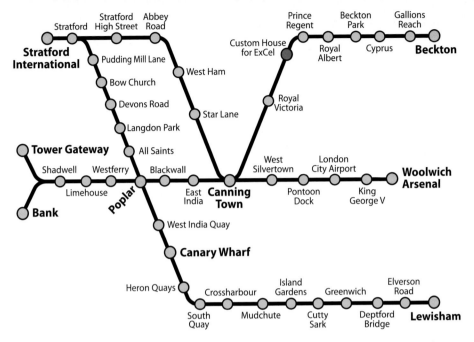

00.18 (M-S), 23.19 (Sun). On weekdays, trains run every five minutes, increased to every four minutes at peak times. At weekends early and late trains run at ten minute intervals, increasing to every five minutes for the majority of the day.

Tower Gateway to Beckton: From Tower Gateway the first trains are: 05.28 (M-S), 06.58 (Sun). Last trains are 23.48 (M-F), 23.49 (Sat), 22.49 (Sun). From Beckton the first trains are: 05.29 (M-S), 06.59 (Sun). Last trains are: 00.29 (M-S), 23.29 (Sun). On weekdays trains run every five minutes, increased to every four minutes at peak times. At weekends trains are every ten minutes for most of the day.

Stratford International to Woolwich Arsenal: From Stratford International the first trains are: 05.30 (M-S), 07.00 (Sun). Last trains are: 00.12 (M-S), 23.11 (Sun). From Woolwich Arsenal the first trains are: 05.27 (M-S), 06.57 (Sun). Last trains are: 00.07 (M-S), 23.07 (Sun). On weekdays trains run every ten minutes, increased to every eight minutes at peak times. At weekends trains are every ten minutes for most of the day.

Stratford to Canary Wharf: From Stratford the first trains are: 05.28 (M-S), 06.55 (Sun). Last trains are: 00.24 (M-S), 23.20 (Sun). From Canary Wharf the first trains are: 05.29 (M-S), 06.51 (Sun). Last trains are: 00.39 (M-F), 00.36 (Sat), 23.36 (Sun). On weekdays trains run every five minutes, increased to every four minutes at peak times. At weekends trains are every five minutes for most of the day, with early and late trains at ten minute intervals.

59 sweeps into Pudding Mill Lane on Stratford branch from Poplar to Stratford, on a short two car 'train'. The construction site on the right hand side is very typical of the Docklands area with its seemingly constant transformation since its inception. This job is part of the Crossrail project. DU

*130 leads a three car 'train' made up of B07 stock into Crossharbour. The newer type of rolling stock used on the DLR has an updated front-end amongst other features but has the added complication that it can only operate with other B07 stock. **DU***

Fares and Tickets

An adult one day travelcard for Zones 1-4 costs £12.30 (£12.10) last year. The DLR is covered by Zones 1 to 4. Woolwich Arsenal is the only DLR station in Zone 4. Single fare journeys can be made using contactless, Oyster and cash. The savings made by using a prepaid card rather than cash are significant as can be shown by this example journey travelling one stop from Bank to Shadwell, from Zones 1 to 2: Oyster and contactless (peak £2.90) off peak £2.40 and cash £4.90, any time.

*Pudding Mill Lane with 79 and 93. This impressive station was built as recently as 2014, when it replaced the previous island platform, slightly further north, from 1996. It is directly opposite the London Stadium, a new 60,000 capacity facility which was built for the Olympics in 2012 and is now the home of Premier League football team West Ham United. **DU***

The Fleet

The DLR operates 149 two-car articulated bi-directional trains:

Built 1991-1992: 23 x Class B90 22 - 44
Built 1992-1995: 47 x Class B92 45 - 91
Built 2002-2003: 24 x Class B2K 92 - 99/01 - 16
Built 2007-2010: 55 x Class B07 101 - 155

The livery carried is uniform across the fleet and is an all-over red with a blue curving stripe to denote the River Thames. The trains usually work as two or three units coupled together. Single unit operation does not normally occur in passenger service. Of note, the B07 stock can only work in multiple with others of the same type, whilst the B90, B92 and B2K stock are all compatible with each other.

Developments

In conjunction with the building of Crossrail, ('Elizabeth Line' as it will be known), Custom House station closed on 3rd February and will not reopen until December 2017. When complete, there will be an interchange here with the new Elizabeth Line.

The 2016 Transport for London Business Plan confirmed that 43 new "full length" trains are to be ordered. This is understood to be the first planned use of a full length train on DLR as opposed to the current practice of two and three car trains running together - with the consequential loss of capacity over the two or four disused front ends. The new full length trains will see a 30% increase in capacity for the same length, using the same platforms. The new trains are expected to enter service in 2022.

In February 2017, TfL announced that the Bakerloo Line is to be extended to Lewisham from its current eastern terminus at Elephant & Castle. Another underground/DLR interchange will be created at Lewisham.

The interchange station at Bank where the DLR meets the Central Line is one of the busiest on the system. At this point DLR is right in the heart of the city. This is the unloading platform where 28 will stop and offload its passengers before using a headshunt behind the photographer. **DU**

Docklands Light Railway

Fleet details:
23 B90, 2-section 6-axle cars built 1991-1992 by BN Construction, Belgium (Bombardier Transportation)
Motors: 2 x 140kw   **Seats:** 52+4

No.	Notes	No.	Notes
22		34	
23		35	
24		36	
25		37	
26		38	
27		39	
28		40	
29		41	
30		42	
31		43	
32		44	
33			

Fleet details:
47 B92, 2-section 6-axle cars built 1993-1995 by BN Construction, Belgium (Bombardier Transportation)
Motors: 2 x 140kw   **Seats:** 52+4

No.	Notes	No.	Notes
45		69	
46		70	
47		71	
48		72	
49		73	
50		74	
51		75	
52		76	
53		77	
54		78	
55		79	
56		80	
57		81	
58		82	
59		83	
60		84	
61		85	
62		86	
63		87	
64		88	
65		89	
66		90	
67		91	
68			

Fleet details:
24 B2K, 2-section 6-axle cars built 1993-1995 by BN Construction, Belgium (Bombardier Transportation)
Motors: 2 x 140kw   **Seats:** 52+4

No.	Notes	No.	Notes
92		05	
93		06	
94		07	
95		08	
96		09	
97		10	
98		11	
99		12	
01		13	
02		14	
03		15	
04		16	

Fleet details:
55 B07, 2-section 6-axle cars built 2007-2010 by Bombardier, Germany
Motors: 2 x 140kw   **Seats:** 52+4

No.	Notes	No.	Notes
101		129	
102		130	
103		131	
104		132	
105		133	
106		134	
107		135	
108		136	
109		137	
110		138	
111		139	
112		140	
113		141	
114		142	
115		143	
116		144	
117		145	
118		146	
119		147	
120		148	
121		149	
122		150	
123		151	
124		152	
125		153	
126		154	
127		155	
128			

Tyne and Wear Metro

Vital Statistics

Opened: 1980
Owner: Nexus
Operator: DB Regio (Nexus from March 2017)
Number of lines: Two
Number of stations/stops: 60
Depot: Gosforth
Route mileage: 46.3 (74.5km)
Power supply: 1500V DC overhead line
Track gauge: 4ft 8½in (1435mm)
Website: www.nexus.org.uk/metro
Passenger journeys: 40.3 million in 2015/16 (+5.7% on 2014/15)
Passenger revenue: £50.2 million in 2015/16 (+4.5% on 2014/15)
Vehicle miles: 3.5 million in 2015/16 (-0.5% on 2014/15)

Timeline

1974: Construction began.

1980-1984: The original system opened in stages and was credited as being the first second-generation light rail system in the UK and the first of today's modern light rail networks in the UK - albeit with no street running.

1991: Bank Foot to Newcastle Airport extension opened.

2002: Pelaw to South Hylton extension opened. This was the first use of shared track operation between light and heavy rail in the UK.

4075 and 4021 top and tail the Rail Head Treatment train on 28th October, passing Hebburn while working train 171 via South Shields. The use of passenger trains/trams on RHTT must be unique to the Tyne and Wear Metro! **Anthony Whiteford**

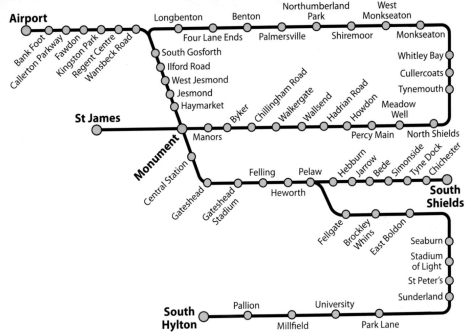

Routes

Two basic services operate:

Green Line: Airport – Monument - South Hylton
Yellow Line: St. James – Monument – North Shields – Monument - South Shields

Timetables

Valid from 05 February 2017:

Green Line: From Airport the first trains are: 05.37 (M-F), 05.39 (Sat), 06.26 (Sun) and the last trains are 00.01 (daily). From South Hylton the first trains are: 06.01 (M-F), 06.06 (Sat), 07.06 (Sun) and the last trains are 23.07 (daily). Mondays to Saturdays, the daytime off peak service is every 12-13 minutes then every hour in the evening, from 17.00. On Sundays, trains are every 15 minutes for most of the day - including the evenings! (This information comes from the official website and is thought to be incorrect. Trains are probably every 15 minutes in the evening daily).

Yellow Line: From St. James the first trains are: 06.13 (M-F), 06.15 (Sat), 07.00 (Sun) and the last trains are 23.09 (daily). From South Shields the first trains are: 05.42 (M-F), 05.48 (Sat), 07.03 (Sun) and the last trains are 23.11 (daily). Mondays to Saturdays, the daytime off-peak service is every 12 minutes, then every hour in the evening from 17.00. On Sundays, trains are every 15 minutes for most of the day until 22.11 then hourly till 23.11. (Again, this hourly weekday evening service is thought to be incorrect).

Fares and Tickets

Metro Day Saver - all zones - £5.00
Metro Child Day Saver - £1.20
Pop Pay As You Go (PAYG) - one zone £1.50, two zones £2.40, all zones £3.10.
Families should buy an Explorer North East Family ticket for £19.50.

4042 and 4063 on Monkwearmouth Bridge in Sunderland on train 2111, a Newcastle Airport to South Hylton journey. The attractive railway bridge is somewhat dwarfed by the even grander road bridge. **Anthony Whiteford**

The Fleet

The Tyne and Wear Metro operates 90 high floor light rail bi-directional 'Metrocars'.

Built 1975: Prototype 2-car units 4001 and 4002
Built 1978-1981: 2-car units 4003 to 4090
1984-1987: 4001 and 4002 were rebuilt
2010-2015: 86 units were refurbished

The units can operate as singles but are normally in pairs. They are categorised as Class 994 EMUs under the Network Rail TOPS numbering system. Units 4001, 4002, 4040 and 4083 were not refurbished in the 2010-2015 period and are no longer compatible with the rest of the fleet. They are described as being 'reserve' units but are out of service at the time of writing.

86 units received a new black livery with yellow doors and end warning panels when they were refurbished. 4001 carries the original 1975 livery style, but with all-yellow doors to conform to rail vehicle accessibility regulations. Units 4002, 4040 and 4083 all carry old advert liveries.

4001 carrying the older style livery leads a two car train into Fellgate on a working to South Hylton on train 102. 4001 is now stored in need of workshop attention. 28th March 2016. **Anthony Whiteford**

Developments

At the end of March 2017 the operation of the system is to be handed over from DB Regio to Nexus.

4007 leads a two car train into Fellgate on a working to South Hylton. The train number is shown on the LED display in the cab window. Most Tyne and Wear trains are used in pairs. 28th March 2016. **Anthony Whiteford**

Manchester Metrolink

Vital Statistics

Opened: 1992
Owner: Transport for Greater Manchester
Operator: RAPT Group (KeolisAmey from July 2017)
Number of lines: Six
Number of stations/stops: 93
Depots: Trafford and Queen's Road
Route mileage: 60 (96.5km)
Power supply: 750V DC overhead line
Track gauge: 4ft 8½in (1435mm)
Website: www.metrolink.co.uk
Passenger journeys: 34.3 million in 2015/16 (+10.1% on 2014/15)
Passenger revenue: £62.4 million in 2015/16 (9.7% on 2014/15)
*Vehicle miles: 7.2 million in 2015/16 (+27.1% on 2014/15)

*Manchester Metrolink mileage figures represent total mileage of each tram 'set' and when one train is formed of two sets, the kilometres travelled will be counted twice. Therefore, figures for the years after 2011/12 are not directly comparable with earlier ones (or with other systems) as the proportion of double sets has increased in recent years. (Info from DfT).

*3016 and a sister car are seen on a Bury via Victoria service on High Street in the city centre. This area, with its cafés and shops, gives the tramway a rather European look. 3016 is seen carrying the advert for Manchester Pride in rainbow colours. 28th August 2016. **David Ardron***

Timeline

1991: Construction began.

1992: The original route from Bury to Altrincham opened, fulfilling the long-held ambition of linking Manchester Piccadilly and Victoria railway stations.

2000: Cornbrook to Eccles opened.

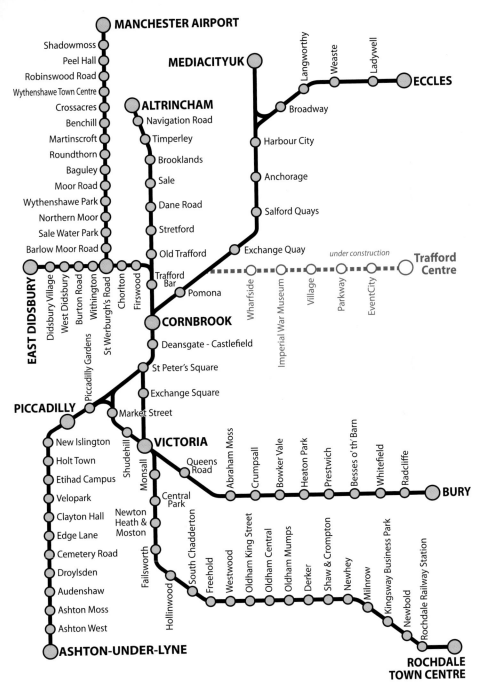

2010: A short spur to Media City was added onto the Eccles route.

2011: Chorlton to St. Werburgh's Road opened.

2012: Former heavy rail line to Oldham Mumps and Shaw and Crompton opened.

2013: Three extensions to East Didsbury, Rochdale and Droylsden (latterly to Ashton-under-Lyne) opened.

2014: Three extensions to Oldham Town Centre, Rochdale Town Centre and Manchester Airport opened.

2016: First part of second city crossing to Exchange Square opened.

2017: Second city crossing fully opened.

3091 is seen heading towards Manchester Airport close to Roundthorn stop in January 2017. A feature of the Metrolink numbering is the use of letters A and B on the actual fleet number, shown on the exterior of the car. It has long been tramway practice of have an A and B end to differentiate the cabs but is very unusual to have this shown on the outside. DU

Routes

As of spring 2017, following the opening of 2CC there are five basic services in operation plus three peak hour Monday to Saturday workings on services A, D and H.

A. Altrincham - Bury
B. Altrincham - Etihad Campus
C. Bury - Piccadilly
D. MediaCityUK - Piccadilly
E. Ashton-under-Lyne - Eccles
F. Manchester Airport - Deansgate - Castlefield
G. East Didsbury - Rochdale Town Centre
H. East Didsbury - Shaw and Crompton

3024 leaves Wythenshawe Park stop, crosses over Wythenshawe Road and is about to head down Moor Road on its way to Manchester Airport on 13th January 2017. This stop is rather neatly situated in a tight space after a near 90 degree curve. DU

Timetable

Such is the scope of the Manchester system, it's impossible to list individual route timetables in detail. It is further complicated as they are split into four periods of operation: Mondays to Thursdays, Fridays, Saturdays and Sundays/Bank Holidays. Full details can be found here: *www.metrolink.co.uk/tramtimes/Documents/metrolink-tram-times-passengers.pdf*

Fares and Tickets

At-stop ticket machines are on all platforms with single, daily, weekly and period tickets available, with the off-peak Day Travelcard offering the best value for exploring the system: Adult £5 (£7 peak), Child £2 (£2.90 peak) and Family £6.20. A Weekend Travelcard allows unlimited travel from after 6pm on Friday until the end of service on Sunday: Adult £5.80, Child £2.70 and Family £8.00. Various Combined Travelcards offer great value for those who wish to also use local buses and trains.

The Fleet

Manchester Metrolink operates 120 two-car articulated bi-directional trams.

Built 2009-2016: 3001 - 3120

All trams are to a high floor specification and carry the standard Metrolink livery of silver and yellow.

They operate singly or pairs. This is the only system in the UK that has platform capacity to hold two trams, on two different services at once. Normal practice at city centre stops is for the tram arriving to load/offload at the front end of the platform, allowing a second to follow in behind. Of the original T68 1000-series and 2000-series fleet, 1007, 1020, 1023 and 2001 are in store at Trafford Park. Trams 1016, 1022, 1024 and 1026 are stored at Long Marston.

As part of the temporary extension of services from Rochdale via Victoria station to Exchange Square, before the full opening of 2CC, trams had to turn back using the crossover situated past the Exchange Square stop. This has now ceased. This stop is outside the busy Arndale shopping centre. **DU**

Developments

New Passenger Record - 3.3 million passengers were carried during the 31 days of October 2016. The previous record was 3.1 million passengers carried in October 2015.

Trafford Park Extension - During October 2016 it was announced that the government has approved the Trafford Park line, which will see a 3.4 mile extension of the system from Pomona (on the current Eccles line) to the Trafford Centre. Assuming that this work will start shortly, opening would be expected in 2020/1.

Sunday 23rd October 2016 saw the last Bombardier M5000 type tram enter service. Also numerically the last, 3120 had only arrived from Vienna on 1st October.

Services ran to Exchange Square (on Corporation Street) for the first time on Sunday 6th December 2016. This section is part of the second city crossing.

Sunday 26th February 2017 saw the opening of the Second City Crossing (2CC), from St Peter's Square to Victoria via Cross Street and Exchange Square. The first tram to operate in passenger service was 3064.

Rarely photographed on any tramway are the maintenance vehicles which help to keep the system safe and operable. These usually work at the quietest times, either at night or weekends. L253HKK is seen here top and tailing a wagon which is used to check and repair the overhead wires. The lift can be seen in front of a pantograph used to check fittings and alignments. **Lee Shaw**

Stagecoach Supertram
Sheffield

Vital Statistics

Opened: 1994
Owner: South Yorkshire PTE
Operator: Stagecoach
Number of lines: Three
Number of stations/stops: 48
Depots: Nunnery
Route mileage: 18 (29km)
Power supply: 750V DC overhead line
Track gauge: 4ft 8½in (1435mm)
Website: www.supertram.net
Passenger journeys: 11.6 million in 2015/16 (+0.6% on 2014/15)
Passenger revenue: £11.4 million in 2015/16 (-10.2% on 2014/15)
Vehicle miles: 1.4 million in 2015/16 (+3.0% on 2014/15)
(Although known by its trading name of Stagecoach Supertram, the official name, as recognised by the DfT, is Sheffield Supertram).

Timeline

1993: Construction began.
1994/1995: The three lines opened.
2018: Sheffield - Rotherham tram-train service due to commence.

Routes

The three longstanding routes continue:
Yellow: Meadowhall to Middlewood
Blue: Malin Bridge to Halfway
Purple: Cathedral to Herdings Park
(extended from Cathedral to Meadowhall off-peak)

Timetable

Yellow route: The first tram from Meadowhall is 05.50 (M-F), 05.48 (Sat), 07.48 (Sun). The last tram is 00.03 (M-S), 23.43 (Sun). The first tram from Middlewood is 05.50 (M-F), 06.06 (Sat), 07.46 (Sun). The last tram is 00.04 (Mon-Sat), 23.44 (Sun). The yellow route service summary is every 10 minutes Mon-Sat peak, every 20 minutes Mon-Sat off-peak and all day Sundays.

Blue route: The first tram from Malin Bridge is

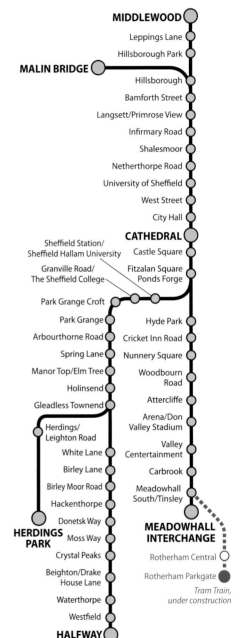

MIDDLEWOOD
Leppings Lane
Hillsborough Park
MALIN BRIDGE
Hillsborough
Bamforth Street
Langsett/Primrose View
Infirmary Road
Shalesmoor
Netherthorpe Road
University of Sheffield
West Street
City Hall
CATHEDRAL
Sheffield Station/ Sheffield Hallam University
Castle Square
Granville Road/ The Sheffield College
Fitzalan Square
Ponds Forge
Park Grange Croft
Park Grange
Hyde Park
Arbourthorne Road
Cricket Inn Road
Spring Lane
Nunnery Square
Manor Top/Elm Tree
Woodbourn Road
Holinsend
Gleadless Townend
Attercliffe
Herdings/ Leighton Road
Arena/Don Valley Stadium
White Lane
Valley Cententertainment
Birley Lane
Birley Moor Road
Carbrook
Hackenthorpe
Meadowhall South/Tinsley
Donetsk Way
HERDINGS PARK
Moss Way
MEADOWHALL INTERCHANGE
Crystal Peaks
Rotherham Central
Beighton/Drake House Lane
Rotherham Parkgate
Tram Train, under construction
Waterthorpe
Westfield
HALFWAY

05.56 (M-F), 05.59 (Sat), 07.59 (Sun). The last tram is 23.52 (M-S), 23.31 (Sun). The first tram from Halfway is 05.57 (M-F), 05.59 (Sat), 07.59 (Sun). The last tram is 00.10 (M-S), 23.51 (Sun). The blue route service summary is every 10 minutes Mon-Sat peak, every 20 minutes Mon-Sat off-peak and all day Sundays.

Purple route: The first tram from Herdings Park is 05.55 (M-F), 05.57 (Sat), 08.02 (Sun). The last tram is 00.01 (M-S), 23.49 (Sun). The first tram from Cathedral is 06.21 (M-F), 06.22 (Sat), 07.39 (Sun). The last tram is 23.26 (M-F), 23.29 (Sat), 23.26 (Sun). The service summary is every 30 minutes Mon-Sat peak, every 20 minutes Mon-Sat off-peak and all day Sundays. Note: empty stock workings are not detailed, but all trams start and finish each day at Nunnery depot.

A rather fortuitous scene at Nunnery Depot on 24th January 2017. Duewag 113 is undertaking several driver training manoeuvres around the depot yard whilst in the background are the new Citylink Tram/Trains. At this time they were stored prior to testing. 399207, 205 and 202 are seen. DU

Fares and Tickets

From 02.01.17. Payable to conductor: Single, daily and weekly tickets available, with the Tram only Dayrider at £3.90 (adult), £2.00 (child) and £9.00 (family) offering good value for exploring the system. For an extra 10p a Tram and Bus Dayrider (Stagecoach buses in Sheffield) is also available for £4.00 (adult). Single fares are split into three very simple categories: Adult single (shorter journeys) £1.60, Adult return (short journey return) £3.00 and Adult Single (longer journeys) £2.30. It is also permitted to break your journey with a single ticket. No Adult return for longer journeys is offered as it is advisable to buy a Dayrider ticket.

The Fleet

Stagecoach Supertram operates 25 three-car double-articulated bi-directional trams and the seven new Class 399 tram-trains will enter service from 2017.

Built 1993-1994: 101 - 125

2006-2009: Mid-life overhauls

Built 2015-2016: 399201 - 399207

The trams carry the Stagecoach Rail division livery of mainly blue with red and orange flares and orange doors. Some cars carry advertising liveries; 120 received a special livery in 2010 to commemorate 50 years since the closure of the original Sheffield tramway system. They only operate as single units.

*103 passing the entrance to Nunnery Depot on a yellow route journey to Middlewood. Rather unusually for light rail in the UK, the Duewags have mirrors; there are four at each end and are a sign of its age, dating back to 1992. **DU***

*122 heading towards the Leppings Lane tram stop on its way to Meadowhall. This stop is the nearest to Hillsborough, the football ground of Sheffield Wednesday. Unfortunately the other football team in the city, Sheffield United is not directly served by the tramway. **DU***

Developments

The order for the 399 class tram/train was placed with Vossloh AG in Spain but partway through producing the order the company became part of Stadler so thereafter the trams were known as Stadler-built products.

2017 saw work progress slowly on the Tram/Train project from Meadowhall South/Tinsley to Rotherham Parkgate. There are signs of construction at Tinsley, where the chord is to be built connecting the tramway with the Tram/Train project. This will see Rotherham Central have low floor platforms and Rotherham Parkgate the new terminus of the

Sheffield's celebrity tram is number 120, painted in the blue and cream carried originally by the Sheffield Corporation Transport trams. One half of this set is the original 120 and the other half is from 118, following a collision. **DU**

tram/train operation. Despite all seven of the expensive and un-tested 399s having been delivered, the project is running behind its intended "early 2017" schedule and has been pushed back to 2018. The first of the tram/train vehicles, 399 201, saw testing progress slowly during the first part of the year, initially between the depot and Shalesmoor (via Sheffield station). 399 201 is believed to have visited the blue route terminus at Halfway.

March 2017 saw notices go up across the system warning passengers of the testing of the new tram/trains across the network.

Tram/Train delivery dates

399201 - 30th November 2015

399202 – 23rd/24th May 2016

399203 - 28th June 2016

399205 - 26th September 2016

399206 - 17th October 2016

399207 - 20th November 2016

105 storms into the sun at the University of Sheffield, emerging from a small subway section. This is a very busy stop. **DU**

First trams from East Croydon are: 04.34 (daily) and the last tram is 00.49 (daily). The basic daily service is every 15 minutes all day.

Line 2: From Beckenham Junction the first trams are: 05.24 (daily) and the last tram is 01.09 (daily). From East Croydon the first trams are: 04.57 (daily) and the last tram is 00.42 (daily). The basic daily service is every 10 minutes during the day, every 15 minutes in the evening.

Line 3: From New Addington the first trams are: 04.53 (daily) and the last tram is 23.53 (daily). From Wimbledon the first trams are: 05.30 (daily) and the last tram is 00.15 (daily). The basic daily service is every 7/8 minutes during the day, every 7/8 minutes during the evening until 21.01 when it becomes every 15 minutes (M-F). Every 7/8 minutes during the day until 20.00 when it becomes every 15 minutes during the evening (Sat and Sun).

Line 4: From Elmers End the first trams are: 06.36 (M-F), 08.06 (Sat and Sun) and the last trams are: 01.10 (daily). From Therapia Lane the first trams are: 04.20 (daily) and the last trams are 19.30 (M-F), 18.30 (Sat), 18.30 (Sun). The basic daytime service is every 15 minutes.

Stadler Variobahn 2554 carries an attractive purple advert for 'Love Croydon'. This section of the tramway in the centre of Croydon is part of the one way single track loop, 4th February 2017. **DU**

Fares and Tickets

Single cash fares at £2.60 per journey (£1.50 with contactless or Oyster) and a £5.00 one-day bus and tram only ticket are available from at-stop ticket machines on all platforms.

You can also travel on the trams if you have a Travelcard either on paper or on your Oyster which includes Zones 3, 4, 5 or 6, or a One Day Bus and Tram Pass either on paper or on your Oyster card.

The Fleet

Tramlink operates 36 two-car articulated bi-directional trams.

Built 1998-1999: 2530 - 2553
2008-2009: All trams were refurbished
Built 2011-2016: 2554 - 2565

The trams carry a lime green, white and blue livery. Some carry advertising liveries. They only operate as single units. At the time of writing tram 2551 was out of service following the incident at Sandilands in November 2016.

2564 arrived at Therapia Lane Depot on 25th September and entered service on 21st October 2016. 2565 arrived on 9th October and entered service on 4th November 2016.

Above: It might not be expected for modern light rail systems to be set in idyllic and pretty locations but the tranquil and leaf covered junction at Arena shows that they can be. Bombardier CR4000 2552 takes the junction on a journey from Beckenham Junction, a very interesting line. **DU**

Below: Stadler 2562 shows off its rather unusual livery at Arena. This tram is the penultimate Stadler to be built and is supposed to show the vehicle being unwrapped at one end! It is heading straight on at the junction on a journey to Elmers End. **DU**

No 35 on a section of reserved track near to Snow Hill. The grass gives this area a very continental feel. **Alan Robson**

The Fleet

Midland Metro operates 21 five-section articulated bi-directional trams.

Built 2013-2015: 17 - 37

The trams carry a silver and pink livery. Some carry advertising liveries. They only operate as single units. The original Ansaldo trams, numbered 01 to 16, are currently stored at Long Marston and Wednesbury depots.

Developments

After several delays and some last minute realignment works, tram services were extended from Bull Street to Grand Central (otherwise known as Birmingham New Street station) on 30th May 2016.

Bull Street tram stop was renamed 'St. Chad's' from January 2017.

Four further CAF Urbos3 trams are currently on order, to service planned extensions; they will take fleet numbers 38-41.

The new Midland Metro Alliance has applied for the Transport and Works Act Order necessary for the Birmingham 'Eastside' extension. This will take trams from Bull Street to Digbeth High Street, just over a mile away, to serve the proposed HS2 station at Curzon Street. Seven additional trams would be acquired to service the extension and capacity growth.

28 is seen among some beautiful architecture on Corporation Street in Birmingham city centre. **Alan Robson**

Left: No 23 is part of the 21-strong Spanish CAF-built Urbos 3 fleet, seen here heading under a railway bridge on its way towards Wolverhampton on Bilston Road. The line here leads to Wolverhampton Steel terminal. **Alan Robson**

Right: Also on Bilston Road is this bridge which passes over Birmingham canal. This is 28 on 15th August 2016. **Alan Robson**

Operational fleet:
21 Urbos 3 5-section 6-axle cars built 2013-2015 by CAF, Spain
Seating: 52 (plus 2) and 154 standing
Equipment: 12 x 80kw motors

No.	Name	Notes
17		
18		
19		
20		
21		
22		
23		
24		
25		
26		
27		
28		
29		
30		
31		
32		
33		
34		
35	Angus Adams	
36		
37	Ozzy Osbourne	

Nottingham Express Transit

Vital Statistics

Opened: 2004
Owner and Operator: Tramlink Nottingham
Number of lines: Two
Number of stations/stops: 51
Depot: Wilkinson Street
Route mileage: 20 (32km)
Power supply: 750V DC overhead line
Track gauge: 4ft 8½in (1435mm)
Website: www.thetram.net
Passenger journeys: 12.2 million in 2015/16
(+50.2% on 2014/15)
Passenger revenue: £13.6 million in 2015/16
(+54.9% on 2014/15)
Vehicle miles: 1.6 million in 2015/16
(+102.1% on 2014/15)
(The large increases are due to the opening of phase two in 2015)

Timeline

2001: Construction began.
2004: Nottingham Railway Station to Hucknall and Phoenix Park opened.
2012: Construction of phase two began.
2015: Nottingham Railway Station to Clifton and Toton Lane opened.

Routes

Although not designated as such, NET uses the line colours of purple and green:

Purple: Phoenix Park – David Lane - Nottingham Station – Toton Lane
Green: Hucknall – David Lane - Nottingham Station – Clifton South

Timetable

Purple line: From Phoenix Park the first tram is 06.04 daily. Mondays to Fridays the service is then every 15 minutes until 07.03; every seven minutes until 10.10; every 10 minutes until 15.02; every seven minutes until 19.10; every 10 minutes until 21.02 then every 15 minutes until 00.15. On Saturdays the service is every 15 minutes until 07.18; every 10 minutes until 10.17; every 7 minutes until 19.10; every 10 minutes until 21.02 then every 15 minutes until

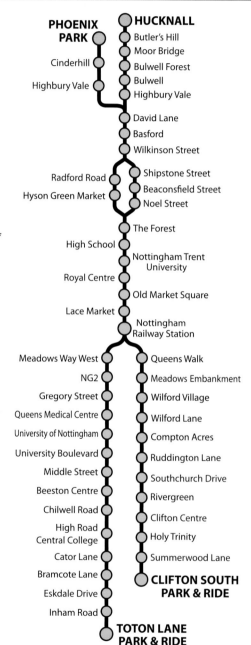

PHOENIX PARK
HUCKNALL
Butler's Hill
Moor Bridge
Cinderhill
Bulwell Forest
Highbury Vale
Bulwell
Highbury Vale
David Lane
Basford
Wilkinson Street
Radford Road
Shipstone Street
Hyson Green Market
Beaconsfield Street
Noel Street
The Forest
High School
Nottingham Trent University
Royal Centre
Old Market Square
Lace Market
Nottingham Railway Station
Meadows Way West
Queens Walk
NG2
Meadows Embankment
Gregory Street
Wilford Village
Queens Medical Centre
Wilford Lane
University of Nottingham
Compton Acres
University Boulevard
Ruddington Lane
Middle Street
Southchurch Drive
Beeston Centre
Rivergreen
Chilwell Road
Clifton Centre
High Road Central College
Holy Trinity
Cator Lane
Summerwood Lane
Bramcote Lane
CLIFTON SOUTH PARK & RIDE
Eskdale Drive
Inham Road
TOTON LANE PARK & RIDE

205 and 232 are seen at Clifton South prior to their next departures to Phoenix Park. The variation in livery and nose-end profiles can clearly be seen here. **DU**

00.15. On Sundays, the service is every 15 minutes until 07.02; every 10 minutes until 19.02 and every 15 minutes until 23.15. From Clifton South, the first tram is 06.02 (daily) and the service operates at almost identical times to above with the last tram 00.48 (M-S), 23.48 (Sun).

Green Line: From Hucknall the first tram is 06.04 daily. The frequency patterns are almost identical to the purple line daily, with the last tram at 00.15 (M-S) and 23.15 (Sun). From Toton Lane the first tram is 06.01 (daily) and again service levels are almost identical daily, with the last tram at 01.05 (M-S), 00.05 (Sun). Trams on both routes start and finish each day at Wilkinson Street depot.

A handful of Nottingham trams carry advert liveries. Here 211 is stabled off-peak on the depot. The irony is not lost that an advert for trams built by Alstom is carried by one built by Bombardier! **DU**

Fares and Tickets

At stop ticket machines: Single, daily and weekly tickets available, with day tickets at £4.00 (adult), £2.20 (child) and £9.00 (Peak Group) offering good value for exploring the system. Nottingham uses a similar system to the London Oyster card called a Mango card, which offers discount on tickets for regular travellers.

Left: *Also stabled off-peak, 231 rests between duties at Wilkinson Street depot. On a normal weekday, about five or six trams are stabled here from 10.30, returning to traffic from 15.30.* **DU**

Right: *The stop at Cinderhill is one of the smallest on the system, sandwiched between two bridges. It is the only one to have a single platform with bi-directional running.* **DU**

The Fleet

NET operates 37 five-section articulated bi-directional trams.

Built 2002-2003: 201 - 215
Built 2014-2015: 216 - 237

The trams carry a silver and turquoise livery with black window surrounds. Some cars carry advertising liveries. They only operate as single units.

A rare shot at The Forest with the centre track being used. Left to right, 217 is working a Clifton South - Phoenix Park journey; 221 is on driver training; 205 is working from Phoenix Park to Clifton South. **DU**

Fleet details:

15 Incentro AT6/5 5-section 6-axle cars built 2002-2003 by Bombardier Transportation, Derby
Seating: 54 (plus 4) and 129 standing
Equipment: 8 x 45kw motors

No.	Name	No.	Name
201	Torvill and Dean	209	Sid Standard
202	D H Lawrence	210	Sir Jesse Boot
203	William "Bendigo" Thompson	211	Robin Hood
204	Erica Beardsmore	212	William Booth
205	Lord Byron	213	Mary Potter
206	Angela Alcock	214	Dennis McCarthy, MBE
207	Mavis Worthington	215	Brian Clough
208	Dinah Minton		

Fleet details:

22 Citadis 302 5-section 6-axle cars built 2012-2013 by Alstom, Barcelona
Seating: 62 and 138 standing
Equipment: 6 x 120kw motors

No.	Name	No.	Name
216	Dame Laura Knight (previously Julie Poulter)	227	Sir Peter Mansfield
217	Carl Froch MBE	228	Local Armed Forces Heroes
218	Jim Taylor	229	Viv Anderson MBE
219	Alan Sillitoe	230	George Green
220	Aprille Jones - Nottingham's Nurse of the Year (previously Kim Helm)	231	Rebecca Adlington OBE
221	Stephen Lowe	232	William Ivory
222	Richard & Michelle Daniels	233	Ada Lovelace
223	Colin Slater MBE	234	George Africanus
224	Vicky McClure	235	David Clarke
225	Doug Scott OBE	236	Sat Bains
226	Jimmy Sirrel and Jack Wheeler	237	Stuart Broad

Timetable

The Edinburgh timetable is very simple. Daily, the first tram is 05.02 from Gyle Centre (the first stop out of Gogar depot) to York Place. It works the 05.30 to the Airport then the 06.18 back to York Place. Monday to Friday, the service is then at least every 10 minutes for an hour then every 7 minutes for the rest of the day. On Saturdays and Sundays the basic service starts the same and is every 10 minutes until 08.03 then every 7 minutes throughout the day until 18.53 when it changes to every ten minutes for the evening. The timetable finishes the same daily, with a 22.48 from Airport to York Place and a 23.30 York Place to Airport; this obviously leaves workings to the depot but these are not shown in the timetable. A Sunday service normally operates on Bank Holidays.

With farmland and open fields, this image from the Ingliston Park and Ride stop seems a million miles away from your typical Airport to City tram system! **Phil Wimbush**

Fares and Tickets

At stop ticket machines on all platforms: Single, return and period tickets are available. The Dayticket – City Zone at £4.00 (adult), £2.00 (child) and £8.50 (family) includes all stops except Edinburgh Airport; The Dayticket – Airport Zone at £9.00 (adult) and £4.50 (child) includes the airport stop. Both tickets are also valid on Lothian Bus services.

The Fleet

Edinburgh Trams operates 27 seven-section articulated bi-directional trams.

Built 2009-2011: 251 - 277

The trams carry a white, red and black livery. They only operate as single units. At seven sections, these trams are the longest to operate in the UK (42.8 metres/140.4 feet). Unlike the majority of other light rail systems, whereas 95% or more of the fleet are required for service daily, Edinburgh Trams only needs nine or ten trams on a daily basis, with the rest spare. All 27 are operational and are used in rotation.

Developments

A new tram and heavy rail interchange close to the tram depot at Gogar and known as Edinburgh Gateway opened in December 2016.

274 approaches Haymarket working a journey to York Place. Note the warning boards that trams are now running. This image dates to 31st May 2014. **Phil Wimbush**

Fleet details:
27 7-section 8-axle cars built 2009-2011 by CAF, Spain
Seating: 78 and 170 standing
Equipment: 12 x 80kw motors

No.	Notes	No.	Notes
251		265	
252		266	
253		267	
254		268	
255		269	
256		270	
257		271	
258		272	
259		273	
260		274	
261		275	
262		276	
263		277	
264			

Blackpool Tramway

Vital Statistics

Opened: 1885 (Traditional)/2012 (LRT)
Owner: Blackpool Council
LRT Operator: Blackpool Transport
Heritage Operator: Blackpool Heritage Tram Tours
Number of lines: One
Number of LRT stations/stops: 38
Number of Heritage stops: Seven
Depots: Starr Gate ('A' fleet) and Rigby Road ('B' and 'C' fleet)
Route mileage: 11.5 (18.5km)
Power supply: 600V DC overhead line
Track gauge: 4ft 8½in (1435mm)
LRT website: www.blackpooltransport.com
Heritage website: www.blackpoolheritage.com/httours
LRT Passenger journeys: 4.9 million in 2015/16 (+20.3% on 2014/15)
LRT Passenger revenue: £6.1 million in 2015/16 (+8.7% on 2014/15)
LRT Vehicle miles: 0.6 million in 2015/16 (+10.3% on 2014/15)
(The Heritage service does not come under the remit of the DfT. Annual passenger numbers, revenue and tram mileages are not published).

Timeline

1884: Construction began.
1885: Line from Victoria (South) Pier to Cocker Street opened.
1898: (North Station) Gynn Square to Fleetwood opened.
1900: Cocker Street to Gynn Square opened.
1903: Victoria Pier to Pleasure Beach opened.
1926: Pleasure Beach to end of South Promenade (near Starr Gate) opened.
1938: End of South Prom to Starr Gate (and loop) opened.
2009: Starr Gate to Pleasure Beach and Ash Street to Fleetwood Ferry closed.
2010: Little Bispham to Ash Street closed.
2011: Last year of traditional trams. Old system closed on 4th November.
2012: Upgraded/rebuilt 'Supertram' system opened on 4th April.

Services

The year-round Starr Gate to Fleetwood service is operated by the Bombardier Flexity2 trams at up to every 10 minutes during the summer and up to every 15 minutes during the winter. This is occasionally supplemented during busy periods of the summer season and autumn illuminations by a small fleet of rebuilt 1930s vehicles which operate as unscheduled 'specials', being directed

FLEETWOOD FERRY
Victoria Street
London Street
Fisherman's Walk
Stanley Road
Lindel Road
Heathfield Road
Broadwater
Rossall Square
Rossall School
Rossall Beach
Thornton Gate
West Drive
CLEVELEYS
Anchorsholme Lane
Little Bispham
Norbreck North*
Norbreck
Sandhurst Avenue
BISPHAM
Cavendish Road
Lowther Avenue
Cabin
Cliffs Hotel
Gynn Square
Wilton Parade
Pleasant Street
NORTH PIER
Tower
Central Pier
Manchester Square
St Chad's Road
Waterloo Road
South Pier
PLEASURE BEACH
Burlington Road West
Harrow Place
STARR GATE

around the system as required. From late January, heritage services operate at weekends and on weekdays during school holidays, throughout the season. The core heritage service runs between Pleasure Beach and North Pier, with selected journeys extended to Cabin, using two heritage trams. Gold heritage weekends (which include bank holiday weekends) feature up to six different heritage trams each day and include tours to Fleetwood. During the autumn illuminations, tours operate from dusk every evening, departing from Pleasure Beach.

Balloon 717 is named after 'Walter Luff' the man responsible for the Streamlined fleet in Blackpool in the 1930s. The popular car is seen at Cabin on a working as part of the heritage operation in 2016. DU

Timetable

Due to the seasonal variations in passenger numbers, the Blackpool system usually has three timetables a year. The winter timetable commences at the end of the Illuminations in early November and ends pre-Easter, with a basic 15 minute service over the whole route daily, every 30 minutes in the evening. The summer timetable runs from Easter until early September, with a basic 10 minute headway during the day daily, then every 30 minutes Starr Gate - Bispham and every 30 minutes Starr Gate - Fleetwood, during the evening, to give a 15 minute promenade service. During the Illuminations, usually late August/early September until early November, a 10 or 12 minute daytime service operates during the day daily, with departures every 7/8 or 10 minutes from Starr Gate in the evening. Two trams per hour run to Fleetwood, the rest terminate at Little Bispham. Generally, year round, the first tram is 05.00 Starr Gate to Fleetwood weekdays, 06.00 Saturdays and 07.00 Sundays. The last tram is 00.15 Fleetwood to Starr Gate, daily. A Saturday service normally operates on Bank Holidays. Blackpool is the only UK system which does not increase capacity during morning/evening peaks. There are no empty stock workings. All trams are in service at all times (except for reverse moves at Starr Gate, Little Bispham etc).

Blackpool has some real gems in its heritage tram collection, which run on selected dates all year round. Fleetwood Box 40 is one of these, dating from 1914 and on loan from the National Tramway Museum. The tram is seen on Hopton Road having just departed Rigby Road depot. DU

Blackpool 'B' fleet car 711 on driver training passes Marton 31, on loan from Beamish Tramway Museum, at Pleasure Beach. **DU**

Fares and Tickets

Payable to conductor: Single, daily, weekly and monthly tickets available, with the Blackpool1 ticket at £5.00 (adult), £2.50 (child) and £10.00 (family) offering good value for exploring the system (valid on all BTS LRT and bus services). These can be purchased online in advance or at a PayPoint store for a discount. Heritage day tickets are available from any conductor (or bus driver), at £11.00 (adult) and £6.00 (child), and offer unlimited travel on the Heritage trams plus all other tram and bus services operated by BTS.

Flexity 004 is seen heading north away from Starr Gate using the crossover, while 005 waits to gain access to the platform at Starr Gate during single line working due to trackwork. **DU**

The Fleet

Blackpool Transport operates a fleet of 16 five-section articulated bi-directional trams ('A' fleet) and five traditional double deckers ('B' fleet) which are modified for the LRT stops, with a further four in store.

Blackpool Heritage Tram Tours operates a fleet of approximately 20 Heritage trams ('C' fleet) with a further 20+ in long term store or under restoration.

A Fleet - Built 2011-2012: 001 - 016
A Fleet - Built 2017: 017 - 018 (to be delivered in 2017)

B Fleet - Built/Rebuilt 1934/1998-2004: 700, 707, 709, 711, 713, 718, 719, 720 and 724
C Fleet - Built 1901 onwards: see table

'A' Fleet trams plus 700, 711 and 719 carry a purple, white, grey and black livery. Some trams carry advert liveries. They only operate as single units. 'B' pool trams mostly carry out-of-contract advert liveries. 'C' pool trams are mostly green and cream with some wearing out-of-contract advert liveries or special liveries.

Friday 29th April 2016 saw the return to service of Balloon car 723 with a special launch tour. The immaculate tram is heading for Fleetwood at North Pier, passing Flexity 015. The mixture of light rail and heritage operation is unique to Blackpool in the United Kingdom. DU

Developments

Funding has been provided for an extension from North Pier to Blackpool North Railway Station. Work will commence in 2017 with an opening date expected around Easter 2019. This will coincide with the electrification of Preston - Blackpool North railway line (expected Easter 2018).

Trams 017 and 018 are expected to be delivered summer 2017 and enter service for the Illuminations.

Ex-towing car 680 was built in 1960 to pull a trailer but has spent the majority of its life operating on its own. The tram is waiting on the Heritage Tram Tours stop on the evening of 13th April 2016, as part of a fish and chip special. The hideous and out-of-place building on the right houses the Tourist Information, a Wedding Chapel and a restaurant/bar. DU

Dublin Luas

Vital Statistics

Opened: 2004
Owner: Transport Infrastructure Ireland
Operator: Transdev
Number of lines: Two
Number of stations/stops: 54
Depots: Red Cow (Red Line) and Sandyford (Green Line)
Route mileage: 24 (38.6km)
Power supply: 750V DC overhead line
Track gauge: 4ft 8½in (1435mm)
Website: www.luas.ie
Passengers carried 2015/2016: Unofficially published as 34.6m*

(Dublin Luas does not come under the remit of the DfT and annual passenger numbers, revenue and tram mileages are not published as per the other systems featured)

Timeline

2000: Construction begins.
2004: The original Green line (June) and Red Line (September) opened.
2009: Extension from Connolly to The Point opened.
2010: Extension from Sandyford to Brides Glen opened.
2011: Branch from Belgard to Saggart opened.
2013: Construction of Green line extension from St Stephen's Green to Broombridge via City Centre began.

Routes

Two unconnected services are operated:

Green Line: St. Stephen's Green – Sandyford – Brides Glen

Red Line: Saggart/Tallaght – Belgard – Busáras – Connolly/The Point

Red line: On weekdays, trams from Saggart operate every 9-10 minutes during peak times and every 10-15 minutes off peak. Trams from Tallaght operate every 4-10 minutes during peak times and every 10-15 minutes off peak. These two routes join up at Belgard where during the peak there is a tram every 3-5 minutes towards Busáras and every 6-15

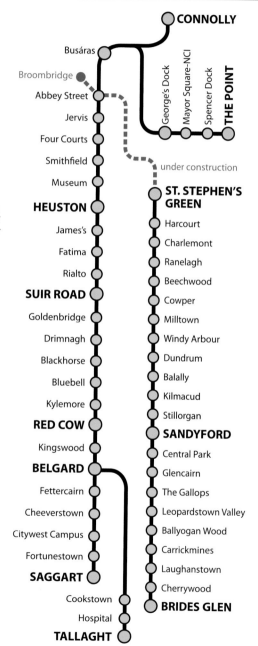

52

minutes off peak. From Busáras to The Point, trams are every 4-10 minutes in the peak and every 10-15 minutes off peak. The single stop Connolly branch has a tram every 9-10 minutes peak, every 10 minutes off peak. The branch closes at 19.00. Weekend services are broadly similar, every 10-12 minutes from both Saggart and Tallaght in the peak and every 12-15 minutes from each off peak. These merge to give a 6-7 minute peak service from Belgard to Busáras on Saturdays, 6-15 minute off peak and a 10-11 minute service on Sundays peak, every 10-15 minutes off peak. From Busáras to The Point, trams are every 10-12 or 12 minutes on weekends during the peak, 11-15 or 12-15 off peak. The branch to Connolly has a limited service every 12 minutes from 09.05 to 18.45 on Saturdays and every 20 minutes from 15.10 to 19.00 on Sundays. The first tram from each terminus is: Saggart - 05.40 (M-F); 06.40 (Sat); 07.10 (Sun). Tallaght - 05.30 (M-F); 06.30 (Sat); 07.00 (Sun). The Point - 05.30 (M-F); 06.30 (Sat); 07.00 (Sun). Connolly - 07.10 (M-F); 09.05 (Sat); 15.10 (Sun). The last tram from each terminus is: Saggart - 23.50 (M-F); 23.50 (Sat); 23.00 (Sun). Tallaght - 00.00 (M-F); 00.00 (Sat); 23.00 (Sun). The Point - 00.30 (M-F); 00.30 (Sat); 23.30 (Sun). Connolly - 19.30 (M-F); 18.45 (Sat); 19.00 (Sun). A Sunday service normally operates on Bank Holidays. Note: Empty stock workings are not detailed, but all trams start and finish each day at Red Cow depot.

Green Line: On weekdays, services from St Stephen's Green as far as Sandyford operate every 3-6 minutes in the peak and every 6-15 minutes off peak. Some are extended to Brides Glen at a frequency of every 4-10 minutes in the peak, every 10-15 minutes off peak. On Saturdays, trams between St Stephen's Green and Sandyford are every 7-8 minutes in the peak and 10-15 minutes off peak and on Sundays, every 11-12 minutes in the peak, 12-15 minutes off peak. In the Sandyford - Brides Glen section, trams are every 13-15 minutes Saturdays peak, 15 minutes off peak and every 11-12 minutes Sundays peak, 12-15 minutes off peak. The first trams from each terminus are: St Stephen's Green - 05.30 (M-F); 06.30 (Sat); 07.00 (Sun). Brides Glen - 05.30 (M-F); 06.30 (Sat); 07.00 (Sun). Sandyford (towards St Stephen's Green) - 05.30 (M-F); 06.30 (Sat); 07.00 (Sun) and Sandyford (towards Brides Glen) - 05.30 (MF); 06.30 (Sat); 07.00 (Sun). The last trams from each terminus are: St Stephen's Green - 00.30 (M-F); 00.30 (Sat); 23.30 (Sun). Brides Glen - 00.00 (M-F); 00.00 (Sat); 23.00 (Sun); Sandyford (towards St Stephen's Green) - 00.15 (M-F); 00.15 (Sat), 23.15 (Sun) and Sandyford (towards Brides Glen) - 00.45 (M-F); 00.45 (Sat); 23.45 (Sun). A Sunday service normally operates on Bank Holidays. Note: Empty stock workings are not detailed, but all trams start and finish each day at Sandyford depot.

An unusual shot of 5004 at St Stephen's Green, the terminus of the Green line. This is not thought to be a designated place to store cycles and use the trams but it appears to be working! **David Ardron**

Passing The Oval pub, this is Abbey Street, right in the heart of Dublin. Here trams run in both directions with road traffic on the left allowed to head east only. 3008 shows off the livery to good effect. **David Ardron**

Fares and Tickets

At-stop ticket machines on all platforms: Single, daily and weekly tickets available, with the Luas Flexi ticket at €7.00 (adult) and €2.90 (child) offering good value for exploring the system.

The Fleet

Luas operates 40 five-section and 26 seven-section articulated bi-directional trams.

Built 2003-2004: 3001 - 3026
Built 2003-2004: 4001 - 4014
Built 2009-2010: 5001 - 5026

The trams carry a silver and yellow livery. They only operate as single units. As there is currently no interworking between the two routes, the 3000 and 4000 series cars exclusively work on the Green line, the 5000 series work the Red line. The 4000 series cars were originally delivered to the Green Line, latterly cascaded to the Red Line when the 5000 series cars were introduced.

Developments

City centre construction work on the Green Line is expected to be completed late-2017. The extension, from the current Green Line terminus at St. Stephen's Green (to Broombridge), will see trams cross the River Liffey on two separate bridges (one new), and will provide connections with the Red Line, which it will cross in Abbey Street. Seven new 54.6 metre long Citadis trams, longer than those currently in use on the Green Line, have been ordered at a cost of €36.5m and are expected to enter service before the end of 2017.

3018 pictured on the two-track terminus at Connolly. The destination screen has already been set for the next journey, back to Tallaght. Until the extension to The Point was built in 2009, this was the western terminus of the Red line. **David Ardron**

3016 approaches Busaras station with a working to Connolly. The tramway passes under the railway here, with Tara Street station just out of view behind the tram. From here commuter services operate to Maynooth, Dundalk, Rosslare Airport and Newbridge. **David Ardron**

Manx Electric Railway
Isle of Man

Vital Statistics

Opened: 1893
Owner: Isle of Man Government
Operator: Isle of Man Railways
Number of lines: One
Depots: Derby Castle and Laxey
Route mileage: 17.75 (28.5km)
Power supply: 550V DC overhead line
Track gauge: 3ft (915mm)
Website: www.gov.im/publictransport

Timeline

1892: Construction began.
1893: Douglas (Derby Castle) to Groudle opened.
1894: Groudle to Laxey opened.
1898: Glen Roy Viaduct completed, line extended to current Laxey station.
1898: Laxey to Ballure opened.
1899: Ballure to Ramsey opened.
1975: Laxey - Ramsey section closed (at the end of the season).
1977: Laxey - Ramsey section reopened.
2007: Laxey - Ramsey section closed (at the end of the season).
2008: A limited service (on 58 days) operated between Laxey and Ramsey.
2009: Laxey - Ramsey section reopened.

Route

The majority of services start and finish at Douglas and run to Ramsey. During certain timetables odd journeys start and finish at Laxey. Until the mid-2000s the service operated all year round but is now seasonal only, usually starting before Easter and finishing in early November. All journeys are timetabled. Specials occasionally run for private hires, enthusiast events and for example, if a cruise ship is visiting the island.

Timetable

Similar to Blackpool, the MER has many peaks and troughs when it comes to passenger loadings, so a preserved railway-style series of letter and colour coded timetables operates. This can be anything from just eight journeys on the low-season timetable A, right through to timetable F which offers a 30 minute all day service, plus an evening service, during the busy TT Race period in June and the Heritage Transport Festival in July. Overall the earliest a tram ever runs is 08.40 from

RAMSEY
Ballure
Belle Vue
Lewaigue
Dreemskerry
Ballajora
Rome's Crossing
Ballafayle (Corteens)
Ballaskeig
Murray's Road / Crowcreen
Cornaa
Ballaglass Glen
Ballagorry
Glen Mona
Ballasholague
Ballig
Ballellin
Dhoon Quarry
Dhoon Glen
Ballaragh
Minorca
Dumbell's Row/ Mines Rd
LAXEY STATION
Laxey Car Shed
South Cape
Fairy Cottage
Ballabeg
Ballagawne
Baldrine
Ballameanagh
Scarffe's Crossing
Halfway House
Eskadale
Groudle Glen
Groudle Old Road/Village
Howstrake
Far End
Braeside
Majestic
Onchan Head
Port Jack
Derby Castle Car Sheds
DOUGLAS DERBY CASTLE

Note: At the start of the 2015 operating season a number of stops, including Walpole Drive, were removed while new ones such as Derby Castle Car Sheds were added. These remain the same in 2017.

Douglas. This journey was introduced following the closure of Ramsey depot to provide a 10.10 Ramsey to Douglas. The last journey of a normal day timetable is 17.40 from Ramsey, but timetable G includes a very late 22.25 from Ramsey, due Douglas at 23.40. This new late journey operated for the first time in 2016.

Another initiative trialled in 2016 which will continue in 2017 is the advertised use of Cars 1 or 2 (the oldest operating tramcars in the world on their original system) on timetable D. This operates on selected days in the summer and 1 or 2 (subject to availability) are booked to work on the 13.40 Douglas to Ramsey and 15.10 return. Details of which timetable runs on which day are beyond the scope of this publication but a well designed and nicely colour coded document can be viewed and downloaded from the IOM government website.

The stars of the MER are undoubtedly cars 1 and 2. This pair of unvestibuled saloons was built in 1893 for the opening of the line. Their claim to fame, as accredited by Guinness World Records, is that they are the oldest tramcars still working on their original line. In 2016 an experiment advertised their use on specific Ramsey timetabled journeys. The pair are seen at Ramsey on 7th June 2016 as part of the increased services which operated during the TT motorbike races. DU

Fares and Tickets

Go Cards are in use for bus and rail journeys with Isle of Man Transport, as well as traditional cash payments on single journeys and 1 Day Go Explore tickets. Single and return tickets are available from the conductor, starting from £4.40 for an adult, although this is for a very short journey and Go Explore tickets offer the best value. An adult return from Derby Castle to Ramsey (the full extent of the line) is £12.40 and £6.20 for a child.

	Adult	Child	Family
1 Day Go Explore	£16.00	£8.00	£39.00
3 Day Go Explore	£32.00	£16.00	£75.00
5 Day Go Explore	£39.00	£19.50	£95.00
7 Day Go Explore	£47.00	£23.50	£115.00

Go Explore cards can be purchased at Derby Castle, Laxey or Ramsey on the MER, the Welcome Centre at the Sea Terminal and Ronaldsway Airport information desk. There is a range of tickets for local residents. The offer of children travelling for free with an adult ticket holder has been withdrawn.

The Fleet

The fleet is split into operational and withdrawn stock. The 2017 operational fleet is expected to comprise 13 motors and 14 trailers, plus nine motors and nine trailers considered as withdrawn, stored or out-of-service. Most of the original rolling stock was delivered between 1893 and 1906 with three new trailers in 1930 and substantial rebuilds to 22 in 1992, 56 in 1995 and 7 in 2010. Most of the fleet carries the red, (brown) and white livery, with three cars in green and white and two in blue and white.

22+47+mail van 16 are seen at the end of Walpole Drive on the approach to Ramsey, about to cross over Queens Drive. Historically the only part of the MER which could be considered as street running, it was stipulated that this section must have side poles; these were originally very ornate and were latterly replaced by the standard basic side poles as seen here. This type of consist was operating as part of the annual Heritage Transport Festival laid on for enthusiasts and the historically accurate combination was very welcome as it shows how the MER used to operate. The Winter saloon, 40-series trailer and mail van were synonymous with the Ramsey line since opening in 1899 until 1975. DU

Developments

At Ramsey, the Goods Shed (built 1899) and the Car Shed (built 1903) were demolished during winter 2016/2017. The station is now closed, pending redevelopment. A temporary station (on the other side of Parsonage Road) will be used during 2017.

Three trams - 21, 32 and 62 - have been painted in green and white livery for 2017 to celebrate the 60th anniversary since the Government takeover of the railways. Trailers 61 and 62 will return to service this year, having last run in 2008. 'Ratchet' Motor 14 is under restoration, due to return in 2018, which is the 125th anniversary of the MER. A week-long celebration is planned for 1st - 8th September.

Tunnel car 5 and trailer 46 at Preston's Crossing on the outskirts of Laxey on their way to Douglas. Car 5 is often referred to as 'The Shrine' due to its internal roof structure. In 1932, it became a unique Tunnel car when it was fitted with 2+1 swingover cushioned seats, replacing the longitudinal benches carried from new and by the rest of the fleet. This changed in 2011 when Car 7 entered service with a similar 2+1 design. DU

Tunnel car 9 was repainted in 2016 and also received new external light bulbs. The trailer here is 58 which returned to service in 2016 following a derailment in 2015 which saw the vehicle fall on its side. The immaculate pairing is seen at the delightfully named Fairy Cottage on their way to Laxey from Douglas. *DU*

6th June 2016 and a scene at Laxey station which has already been confined to the history books! 16+60 carry a version of the green livery worn by various cars upon nationalisation of the MER in 1958, whilst 32+47 look on from the station siding. These cars have swapped liveries for 2017 with only 47 looking as it did here. 32 has been painted in green and white whilst 16+60 are in red and white! **DU**

Fleet details:
24 4-axle bogie single deck motor cars built 1893-1906/1992
Seats: Various
Equipment: Various

No.	Built/Rebuilt	Seats	Type	Notes
1	Built 1893	34	Unvestibuled Saloon	
2	Built 1893	34	Unvestibuled Saloon	
5	Built 1894	32	Tunnel car	
6	Built 1894	34	Tunnel car	
7	Rebuilt 2010	32	Tunnel car	
9	Built 1894	34	Tunnel car	
14	Built 1898	56	Open Crossbench 'Ratchet'	Overhaul in progress
15	Built 1898	56	Open Crossbench 'Ratchet'	Stored
16	Built 1898	56	Open Crossbench	
17	Built 1898	56	Open Crossbench 'Ratchet'	Stored
18	Built 1898	56	Open Crossbench 'Ratchet'	Stored
19	Built 1899	48	Winter Saloon	
20	Built 1899	48	Winter Saloon	
21	Built 1899	48	Winter Saloon	
22	Rebuilt 1992	48	Winter Saloon	
25	Built 1898	56	Open Crossbench	Stored
26	Built 1898	56	Open Crossbench	Stored
27	Built 1898	56	Open Crossbench	Stored
28	Built 1904	56	Open Crossbench 'Ratchet'	Stored
29	Built 1904	56	Open Crossbench 'Ratchet'	Stored
30	Built 1904	56	Open Crossbench 'Ratchet'	Stored
31	Built 1904	56	Open Crossbench 'Ratchet'	Stored
32	Built 1906	56	Open Crossbench	
33	Built 1906	56	Open Crossbench	

Fleet details:
23 4-axle bogie single deck trailer cars built 1893-1906/1930
Seats: Various
Equipment: None

No.	Built/Rebuilt	Seats	Type	Notes
36	Built 1894	44	Crossbench	Stored
37	Built 1894	44	Crossbench	Stored
40	Built 1930	44	Crossbench	
41	Built 1930	44	Crossbench	
42	Built 1903	44	Crossbench	Stored
43	Built 1903	44	Crossbench	
44	Built 1930	44	Crossbench	
46	Built 1899	44	Crossbench	
47	Built 1899	44	Crossbench	
48	Built 1899	44	Crossbench	
49	Built 1893	44	Crossbench	Stored
50	Built 1893	44	Crossbench	Stored
51	Built 1893	44	Crossbench	
53	Built 1893	44	Crossbench	Stored
54	Built 1893	44	Crossbench	Stored
55	Built 1904	44	Crossbench	Stored
56	Rebuilt 1995	18	Saloon*	[A]
57	Built 1904	32	Unvestibuled Saloon	
58	Built 1904	32	Unvestibuled Saloon	
59	Built 1895	18	Unvestibuled Saloon	
60	Built 1896	44	Crossbench	
61	Built 1906	44	Crossbench	Overhaul in progress
62	Built 1906	44	Crossbench	Overhaul in progress

Notes:
[A] *This tram was originally a Crossbench trailer (built 1904) but was converted in 1994/95 to a Saloon Trailer with a dedicated area to convey passengers in wheelchairs. It was fitted with a mechanical lift for loading/unloading.*

Works Cars:

No.	Built/Rebuilt	Seats	Type	Notes
1	Rebuilt 1998		Overhead Tower Wagon	
3	Built 1894		6 ton van	Stored
4	Built 1894		6 ton van	
8	Built 1897/8		6 ton open wagon	
10	Built 1897/8		6 ton open wagon	
11	Built 1898/9		6 ton van	Stored
12	Rebuilt 1977		Overhead Tower Wagon/van	Stored
13	Built 1903/4		Small van	Stored
16	Built 1908		Large mail van	
21	Rebuilt 1926		Flat wagon	
26	Rebuilt 1918		Enclosed Freight Trailer	Stored
34	Rebuilt 2003		Locomotive	
45	Rebuilt 2004		Flat wagon	
52	Rebuilt 2008		Tower wagon	

Snaefell Mountain Railway
Isle of Man

Vital Statistics

Opened: 1895
Owner: Isle of Man Government
Operator: Isle of Man Railways
Number of lines: One
Depot: Laxey
Route mileage: 4.9 (7.8 km)
Track gauge: 3ft 6in (1067mm)
Line voltage: 550V DC overhead line
Website: www.gov.im/publictransport

Summit
Bungalow

Laxey

Route

Services have always run to a similar pattern since inception. Although the pattern is seasonal (mid-March to early-November), the railway operates to a colour coded timetable in a similar style to the Manx Electric Railway. In previous years it just ran to demand with no set timetable. Services are simply Laxey to Summit and return. The busiest time is during the TT races, during which the railway is split into two halves. Services run from Laxey to Bungalow and from Bungalow to Summit, with passengers using a footbridge over the A18 Mountain Road. This normally involves three or four trams on the lower section and one or two trams on the upper, operating on separate tracks.

Timetables

The first passenger journey of the day normally connects with the arrival of the first tram from Douglas, departing five minutes later. This is 10.15 for most of the year. After this trams are usually every 30 minutes with the last departure from Laxey at 15.45. They normally have a 25 minute layover at the Summit, with the last one back at 16.40. Journey time is 30 minutes. Late evening journeys never operated historically, although this has changed recently following the introduction of themed dinner events at the Summit cafe. On a number of dates in 2017, there are 18.25 and 19.25 departures from Laxey, 20.50 and 21.50 from the Summit, which connect at Laxey for late trams to Douglas (and on the 20.50, to Ramsey). When the themed dinner events began, non-dining passengers were able to travel on the trams (using their Explorer passes or buying ordinary return tickets) but this has now ceased - making them exclusively for diners. If you want to travel up the Mountain in the evening you have to pay the full dining fare, even if you don't want to dine!

Fares and Tickets

Douglas to Snaefell adult return is £14.00, child £7.00. The offer of children travelling for free with an adult ticket holder has been withdrawn. See MER section for details of Go Explore tickets.

The Fleet

Cars 1, 2, 5 and 6 are expected to run during 2017. Car 4 is undergoing an overhaul. Most of the fleet carries the red, brown and white livery, with car 1 in blue and white.

A scene which epitomises what the Snaefell Mountain Railway is all about. A gorgeous sunny clear day to enjoy the views. Car 5 is seen heading down the left hand track, for descending cars, another Snaefell anomaly, along with the fell rail, used in emergencies but once used as part of the service brake. 22nd May 2016. DU

Snaefell 1 passes MER cars 19+43, which are in the process of running round on a viciously tight crossover. The Great Laxey Wheel can be glimpsed in the background. The difference in gauges is readily apparent in this view. Snaefell is 3ft 6in and the MER is 3ft. 25th July 2016. **Phil Wimbush**

The terminus at Laxey is shared by the MER and Snaefell Mountain Railway. MER cars 2+43 deliver another load of passengers from Douglas, some of whom will transfer to the SMR car for their onward journey. SMR cars 5 and 2 are seen; 2 carries the new head, tail and side lights, making it suitable for evening service. 21st May 2016. DU

Developments

On 30th March 2016, Snaefell car 3 was involved in a serious incident which saw the tram run away from the Summit down the ascending line (wrong line). There were no passengers or crew on board. Gaining speed rapidly, it derailed on a sharp curve prior to reaching Bungalow, toppling over before rolling a number of times. Dating from 1895 and in largely original condition, the tram was completely smashed to pieces, beyond all recognition. The trucks, electrical equipment and some other parts were recovered in difficult circumstances on the mountainside. The subsequent investigation found that operating circumstances and bad practices (not in the rule book) were to blame. Several improvements, engineering recommendations and record keeping rules were introduced before the service could commence again. A replacement for car 3 is expected to be built in the future.

Fleet details:
6 bogie saloon cars built in 1895 by G.F. Milnes, Birkenhead
Seats: 48
Equipment: Kiepe 4 x 50kw motors

No.	Built	Notes
1	1895	Heavily rebuilt between 2010 and 2013
2	1895	
4	1895	Overhaul in progress
5	1971	Largely destroyed by fire, 1970. Rebuilt by H.D. Kinnin (Ramsey), 1971
6	1895	

Douglas Bay Horse Tramway
Isle of Man

Vital Statistics

Opened: 1876
Owner: Isle of Man Government
Operator: Isle of Man Railways
Number of lines: One
Car depot: Strathallan Crescent (Derby Castle)
Horse stables: Summer Hill Road
Route mileage: 1.6 (2.6km)
Track gauge: 3ft (914mm)
Website: www.douglas.gov.im

> *This is the current terminus of the line which is now referred to as Sea Terminal

Route

A very basic out-and-back service operates from Derby Castle to the roundabout near to the Sea Terminal, known as Victoria Pier. Official publicity states that trams run to the Sea Terminal itself but this is incorrect. The short section from Victoria Pier to the Sea Terminal was closed many years ago and the rails, still in situ, were completely buried in Tarmac more recently. All intermediate crossovers have been removed, leaving no options for short workings.

Sea Terminal ○
*Victoria Pier ○
Gaiety Theatre ○
Broadway ○
Palace Hotel Casino ○
Hydro Hotel ○
Strathallan Crescent ○
(Stables)
Derby Castle ○

*Car 42 is seen just after arrival at the Sea Terminal (Victoria Pier) with passengers unloading whilst 'Charles' waits patiently. The conductor holds the stool which the driver sits on; with only one per tram, it is moved from one end to the other at terminal points. 42 dates from 1905 and was lengthened in 1938, which may account for the car's acquired droop over the years. **DU***

The Douglas Bay Horse Tramway's 'Royal tram' is number 44 which carries this special livery and a brass plaque which details its royal exploits. The popularity of the horses with people of all ages is obvious here. Note the word 'Corporation' on the lower panels has been painted out to leave just Douglas Tramways, following the takeover by Isle of Man Railways! **Chris Pulling**

Fleet details:
19 2-axle horse drawn cars built 1883-1913 by various manufacturers

No.	Built	Type	Notes
1	1913	Enclosed saloon	
12	1888	Open Toastrack	Returned to service on last day of service in 2014
18	1883	Double Deck	Ex-South Shields. Oldest operable tram car.
21	1890	Open Toastrack	
27	1892	Enclosed Saloon	Overhaul in progress
29	1892	Enclosed Saloon	
32	1896	Crossbench	
36	1896	Crossbench	Overhaul in progress
38	1902	Open Toastrack	
42	1905	Open Toastrack	Special livery, similar style to 44. Red and blue.
43	1907	Crossbench	
44	1907	Crossbench	Special livery, Royal Tram. Red and blue.
45	1908	Crossbench	

Volk's Electric Railway
Brighton

Vital Statistics

Opened: 1883
Owner and Operator: Brighton & Hove City Council
Depot: Halfway (Paston Place)
Route mileage: 1.25 (2.0km)
Power supply: 110V DC third rail
Track gauge: 2ft 8½in (825mm)
Website: www.volkselectricrailway.co.uk

Palace Pier
Aquarium Station
Halfway (Paston Place)
Black Rock Station

Route

The railway operates along the seafront, following Madeira Drive from Palace Pier to Black Rock. Similar to Douglas Horse trams, the official map for this system shows services as running Palace Pier - Aquarium - Halfway - Black Rock but the official website only shows times and fares in the Aquarium - Black Rock section.

Timetable

Due to building works, dates of operation were not confirmed as of March. Services usually start around Easter but will begin later in 2017. When it does commence this service is expected to operate: Trains start at 10.15 except on Mondays and Fridays when they start at 11.15. Trains run every 15 minutes after starting, at half past, quarter to, on the hour and quarter past until the last train of the day. Last trains are at 17.00 Monday to Friday and at 18.00 on weekends and Bank holidays. Train times are the starting times from the end stations, Aquarium Station and Black Rock (Marina) Station. Check website for details.

Tram 9, dating from 1910, is seen at the Black Rock terminus of the line. **James Millington**

A coupled set led by car 6 enters the passing loop at the Halfway Station. **James Millington**

Fares

Fares for 2017 were not available at the time of writing. The full trip return fares for 2016 were priced at: £3.70 (adult), £2.80 (senior), £2.20 (child), £9.50 (family).

The Fleet

At the time of writing, cars 4, 6 and 10 were located at a contractor in Ross-on-Wye, undergoing major overhauls. Car 3 is being rebuilt by VER. The service will be operated by the other three cars when it starts. Most of the fleet carries the yellow and brown livery.

Developments

The Volk's Electric Railway had a significant winter upgrade funded by a £1.65million Heritage Lottery Fund grant, entitled 'Saving Volk's'. This has seen a new visitor centre, conservation workshop and refurbished carriages.

Fleet details:
7 2-axle single deck cars built 1892-1926 by VER, Brighton
Seating: 40
Equipment: 1 x 6kw motor

No.	Built	Type	Notes
3	1892	Semi-Open	Withdrawn. Overhaul in progress
4	1892	Semi-Open	Withdrawn. Overhaul in progress
6	1901	Semi-Open	Withdrawn. Overhaul in progress
7	1901	Semi-Open	
8	1901	Semi-Open	
9	1910	Open	
10	1926	Open	Overhaul in progress

Seaton Tramway

Vital Statistics

Opened: 1970
Owner and Operator: Modern Electric Tramways Limited
Depot: Riverside
Route mileage: 3 (4.8km)
Power supply: 120V DC overhead line
Track gauge: 2ft 9in (825mm)
Website: www.tram.co.uk

○ COLYTON

○ Colyford

SEATON ○

Route

The railway runs on the trackbed of the former Seaton to Seaton Junction branch line, following the River Axe from Seaton itself to Colyton.

Timetables

The tramway operates a colour coded service, with four different timetables, depending on the time of year. The yellow service is for early/late season, starting in February, with a tram every 30 minutes. The pink service is for peak summer, with a tram every 20 minutes. On all operating days the service starts at 10.00, with the last round trip from Seaton at 16.00 (yellow) and 17.00 (all others).

No.16, a rebuild of former Bournemouth car 106, awaits more passengers at Seaton Terminus on 27th September 2016. **Phil Wimbush**

Seen at Colyton, no 10 is one of the more recently built cars, dating from 2002 and carrying a livery based on the Glasgow system. *Phil Wimbush*

Fares

Tickets can be booked online in advance or purchased from booking offices at each end of the line. The All Day Explorer ticket at £11.00 (adult), £8.25 (child) and £33.00 (family) offers the best value for exploring the tramway.

The Fleet

A variety of trams are operated. All are serviceable, except car 17 (see below). Various liveries are carried.

Developments

Crossbench tram 17, which was constructed in 1988 to resemble one of the famous trams of the Manx Electric Railway, is being converted into an enclosed saloon. No.17 was unique at Seaton, being the only crossbench single decker.

A £1million donation, received from the widow of a former chairman of the tramway, will be used towards the full redevelopment of the terminus at the Seaton end of the line. It is expected to be a modern development, to complement the surrounding buildings. At Colyton, the Victorian style terminus and period 'street scene' will be retained.

Fleet details:

13 4-axle single or double deck cars built (or rebuilt) 1956-1998 by Modern Electric Tramways, Eastbourne and Seaton, or 2002 by Bolton Trams Ltd, Salford
Seating: Various
Equipment: Various

No.	Built	Notes
2	1964	Metropolitan Electric Tramways style bogie double deck
4	1961	Blackpool Open Boat bogie single deck
6	1954	Llandudno & Colwyn Bay style bogie double deck
7	1958	Llandudno & Colwyn Bay style bogie double deck
8	1968	Llandudno & Colwyn Bay style bogie double deck
9	2002	Plymouth and Blackburn bogie double deck cars
10	2002	Plymouth and Blackburn bogie double deck cars
11	2002	Plymouth and Blackburn bogie double deck cars
12	1966	London Feltham bogie double deck
14	1904/1984	Ex-Metropolitan Electric Tramways no.94
16	1921/1992	Ex-Bournemouth no.106
17	1988	Manx Electric Railway crossbench single deck. Rebuild in progress
19	1906/1998	Ex-Exeter no.19

Great Orme Tramway
Llandudno

Vital Statistics

Opened: 1902

Owner and Operator: Conway County Borough Council

Depot: Victoria Station, Halfway, Summit

Route mileage: 1.25 (2.0km)

Power supply: Cable haulage

Track gauge: 3ft 6in (1067mm)

Website: www.greatormetramway.co.uk

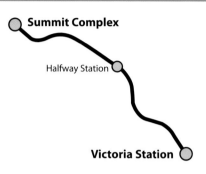

The Route

The tramway is divided into two separate and unconnected sections. The lower part begins at Victoria Station on Church Walks and ends at Halfway Station. It resembles a traditional tramway operating either on, or alongside, the public highway. Departing from Halfway Station on a level grade, the upper section features open reserved track throughout.

Timetables

The official timetable and operating dates are quite vague. Information on the website reads: What time of year does the Tramway run? Late March to late October (for exact dates please call or email us). How many days of the week does it operate? 7 days a week. What time of day? 10am to 6pm (We close at 5pm during March and October). The service is thought to operate at 30 minute intervals when it does run.

For most people the journey on this tramway starts here at the delightful Victoria Station. **Mike Smith**

The upper section of the Great Orme tramway with No.7 heading to Halfway. Note the windowless tram. **David Ardron**

National Tramway Museum
Crich

Vital Statistics

Established: 1959
Opened: 1963
Owner and Operator: The Tramway Museum Society
Route mileage: Approximately 1 (1.6km)
Power supply: 550V DC overhead line
Gauge: 4ft 8½in (1435mm)
Address: Crich Tramway Village, Matlock, DE4 5DP
Website: **www.tramway.co.uk**

GLORY MINE

Wakebridge

Entrance/Bandstand

DEPOT

TOWN END

Timeline

1959: Established on the site of George Stephenson's mineral railway.
1963: First public service operated from Town End to a point close to the depots using horse cars.
1964: First electric services operated.
1966: Line extended to 400 yards in length.
1968: Extension to Wakebridge opened.
1978: Extension to Glory Mine opened.
1991: New exhibition hall opened.
2002: Workshops expanded.
2010: Exhibition hall revamped.
2011: The original Stephenson Workshop reopened following restoration.

Leeds 180, complete with period adverts, is passed by Liverpool 'Liner' 869 which was providing a driving experience. **Phil Wimbush**

On selected days Crich runs horse cars in between its normal electric tramcars. Sheffield 15, dating to 1874 and seating only 16, is seen crossing over outside the depot and pulled by 'Joseph' while Blackpool 166 waits in the background. 26th June 2016. **Jason Cross**

The Route

The line begins at Town End and consists of double track for the first part of its length along the museum's recreated main street. Beyond the depot, the tramway narrows to a short section of interlaced track beneath the Bowes-Lyon bridge, before opening up to double track again by the bandstand. Becoming reserved sleeper track beyond this point, double track ends prior to Cabin Crossing and token working is in place on the single line section to the halfway passing point at Wakebridge. From here to the terminus at Glory Mine, the tramway is single track again and protected by token working. Glory Mine terminus features a passing loop and reversing stub.

Opening Times

The museum is open daily from Saturday 18th March until Sunday 5th November. The annual Tram Day (aimed at enthusiasts) is planned for Saturday 16th September.

Admission Prices

Adult: £16.50, **Senior Citizen:** £12.50, **Child:** £9.50. **Family 2 adults/3 children:** £39.50. All admission tickets are valid for a full year from the date of issue.

Tram Fleet 2017

At the beginning of each year the NTM releases a list of trams which it plans to operate during the forthcoming year. This is awaited with some anticipation by enthusiasts as trams can quickly come and go; releasing the information means that the chance for a farewell to people's favourites are often missed. The list for 2017 has seen the impressive London Transport 1622 withdrawn from service (initially planned for 2016) along with Glasgow open topper 1068. However a more positive note is the return to traffic of Glasgow 22. This leaves 18 electric tram cars and one horse tram expected to be operational in 2017. See fleet list.

Sheffield 510 is seen, once again outside the depot. As it proclaims 510 was Sheffield's last tram, back in 1960. The new system opened in 1994. **Jason Cross**

Developments

Glasgow 22, Blackpool Standard 40 and LCC 106 returned to service during 2016 following overhauls.

Chesterfield Horse car 8 was officially transferred to the NTM during summer 2016.

Restoration of London County Council No.1 'Thunderbird' continued throughout 2016.

Oporto Coal car C65 was moved from store at Clay Cross and transported to Crich as part of the annual Tram Day on 10th September 2016. Afterwards it moved to new owner Beamish Museum which intends to restore it to operational condition.

The National Tramway Museum makes great efforts to represent the different types of tram cars which have operated in Britain through the years. This is fully illustrated here with two types of Blackpool tram - 'Pantograph' car 167 and Blackpool 'Jubilee' 762. 762 is a development of rebuilding a Balloon car (formerly 251/714) into a high-capacity one person operated tram. The livery is somewhat garish but is the only correct scheme for its current condition. **Phil Wimbush**

Fleet details:

No.	Origin	Built	Status
1	Derby	1904	Static display
1	Douglas Head Marine Drive	1896	Static display
1	Glasgow (works car)	1905	Stored (Clay Cross)
1	Leamington & Warwick	1881	Static display
1	London Transport	1932	Undergoing restoration
2	Blackpool & Fleetwood	1898	Static display
2	Blackpool (railgrinder)	1935	Stored (Clay Cross)
2	Leeds (tower car)	1932	Static display
4	Blackpool Electric Tramway Co.	1885	Static display
5	Blackpool	1972	Stored (Clay Cross)
5	Gateshead & District	1927	Static display
7	Chesterfield	1904	Operational for 2017
8	Chesterfield	1904	Static display
9	Oporto	1873	Static display
10	Hill of Howth	1902	Static display
14	Grimsby & Immingham	1915	Static display
15	Sheffield (horse car)	1874	Operational for 2017
21	Cardiff	1886	Static display
21	Dundee & District	1894	Static display
21	Glasgow (stores van)	1903	Stored (Clay Cross)
22	Glasgow	1922	Operational for 2017
35	Edinburgh	1948	Static display
39	North Metropolitan Tramways Co.	unk	Static display (one side as a display case in exhibition hall)
40	Blackpool & Fleetwood	1914	Operational, on loan to Blackpool Transport
40	Blackpool	1926	Operational for 2017
45	Southampton	1903	Static display
46	Sheffield	1899	Stored (Clay Cross)
47	New South Wales Govt.	1885	Static display
49	Blackpool	1926	Static display
59	Blackpool	1902	Stored (Clay Cross)
60	Johannesburg	1905	Static display
74	Sheffield	1900	Operational
76	Leicester	1904	Static display
84	MBRO	1886	Stored (in parts). (Clay Cross)
102	Newcastle	1901	Static display
106	London County Council	1903	Operational for 2017
107	Leeds	1898	Static display
131	Cardiff (water car)	1905	Operational
132	Kingston-upon-Hull	1910	Static display. On loan to Hull Streetlife Museum
159	London United Tramways	1901	Operational for 2017
166	Blackpool	1927	Operational for 2017
166	Nottingham	1920	Stored (Clay Cross)

Fleet details:

No.	Origin	Built	Status
167	Blackpool	1928	Operational for 2017
180	Leeds	1931	Operational for 2017
180	Prague	1908	Static display
184	North Metropolitan (horse car body)	c1895	Stored (in parts)
189	Sheffield	1934	Static display
236	Blackpool	1934	Operational for 2017
249	Blackpool	1935	Static display
264	Sheffield	1937	Static display
273	Oporto	1927	Operational for 2017
298	Blackpool	1937	Stored (Clay Cross)
330	Sheffield	1919	Operational
331	Metropolitan Electric Tramways	1930	Operational for 2017
345	Leeds	1921	Operational for 2017
399	Leeds	1926	Operational for 2017
510	Sheffield	1950	Operational for 2017
600	Leeds	1954	Stored (Clay Cross)
602	Leeds	1953	Static display
630	Blackpool	1937	Operational for 2017
674	New York 3rd Ave. Transit	1939	Static display
762	Blackpool	1982	Operational for 2017
812	Glasgow	1900	Static display
869	Liverpool	1936	Operational for 2017
902	Halle	1969	Static display
1068	Glasgow	1919	Static display
1100	Glasgow	1928	Stored (Clay Cross)
1115	Glasgow	1929	Static display
1147	The Hague	1957	Static display
1282	Glasgow	1940	Static display
1297	Glasgow	1948	Static display
1622	London Transport	1912	Static display
223 006-4	Berlin	1969	Operational for 2017
Loco (717)	Blackpool (works car)	1927	Operational
TW4	Crich (tower wagon)	2011	Operational
58	Croydon Tramlink (works car)	1978	Operational
61	Croydon Tramlink (flatbed trailer)	1978	Operational

Heaton Park Tramway
Manchester

Vital Statistics

Established: 1980
Owned and Operated by: Manchester Transport Museum Society
Route mileage: Approximately 0.5 (0.8km)
Power supply: 550V DC overhead line
Gauge: 4ft 8½in (1435mm)
Address: Heaton Park, Manchester, M25 2SW
Website: www.heatonparktramway.org.uk

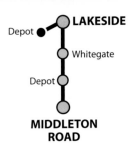

The Route

From Middleton Road gates the route takes a straight line double track alignment to the museum and depot over the surviving tracks of the former Manchester Corporation system. Beyond here, more recent extensions take trams on a single track route which turns right onto the park drive and then left onto reserved track through woodland towards Whitegate. The reservation continues beside the park drive to Old Lakeside, where the drive is crossed at near right angles. Trams then turn left to terminate at Lakeside, beyond which lies the second and newer of the two depots.

Opening Times

The tramway is in operation every Sunday from 19th February until late-November. Special events are held throughout the year - check website for details.

Fares

Payable to conductor

Adult: £2.00 return, £5.00 multi-ride. **Child:** £1.00 return, £2.50 multi-ride.

Family (2 adults and 2 children): £5.00 return, £12.00 multi-ride.

Developments

Sunday 2nd April sees the tramway celebrate 50 years since the Manchester Transport Museum Society was formed.

No.	Origin	Built	Status
			Fleet details:
5	Stockport	1901	Undergoing repairs. On loan from Stockport 5 Tramcar Trust
23	Rawtenstall	1912	Stored (in parts). Awaiting restoration
43	Oldham	1902	Stored. Awaiting restoration
96	Hull	1901	Operational
173	Manchester	1901	Static display
619	Blackpool	1987*	Operational
623	Blackpool	1937	Operational
702	Blackpool	1935	Stored
752	Blackpool (Railgrinder)	1920	Stored
765	Manchester	1914	Operational
L53	Manchester (horse car)	c.1880	On loan to Bury Transport Museum

Two of Heaton Park's longstanding cars pose side by side opposite the depot. 2017 marks 50 years since the MTMS was formed. **DU**

Beamish Museum
County Durham

Vital Statistics

Established: 1970
Owned and Operated by: Beamish Museum Limited
Route mileage: Approximately 1.5 (2.4km)
Power supply: 550V DC overhead line
Gauge: 4ft 8½in (1435mm)
Address: Beamish Museum, Beamish, County Durham, DH9 0RG
Telephone: 0191 370 4000
Website: www.beamish.org.uk

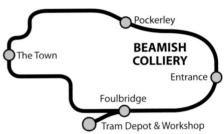

Timeline

1973: Tramway opened.
1988: Tramway extended to museum entrance.
1993: Tramway extended to operate full circuit.

The Route

The tramway is a circular route which is operated in both clockwise and anti-clockwise directions. Clockwise from the passing loop at the museum entrance, the tramway descends a gradient along single track towards the tram depot at Foulbridge, where another passing loop is provided. From here, trams continue on single track again to the recreated town, where double track is provided throughout. A crossover features in the town street, but is rarely used in normal operation. From the town, trams head towards the entrance on a single track alignment to Pockerley, where a further passing loop is provided. The final section of single line between here and the museum entrance is on a steep gradient and is controlled by railway style token block working to ensure safe operation.

Sheffield 264 passing Sunderland 16 at Pockerley. The trams have to collect a token for operating up the steep single line Pockerley bank on their way to the entrance. Sheffield 264 returned to service in 2016 following a full overhaul. **Phil Wimbush**

87

East Anglia Transport Museum
Carlton Colville

Vital Statistics

Operated by: East Anglia Transport Museum Society Limited
Route mileage: Approximately 0.25 (0.4km)
Power supply: 550V DC overhead line
Gauge: 4ft 8½in (1435mm)
Address: Chapel Road, Carlton Colville, Lowestoft, NR33 8BL
Website: www.eatransportmuseum.co.uk

Timeline

1972: Museum opened with 200 yard tramway.
1982: Extension to Hedley Grove opened.

The Route

From the double track stub terminus at Chapel Road, trams run along a recreated street to the left of the three track tram depot then past the front of the adjacent trolleybus depot. Then the track turns sharply left onto a reserved section through woodland, before terminating at Hedley Grove, where a passing loop is provided.

Opening Times

The museum is open on various dates from April to October, check website for details.

Admission Prices

Adult: £9.00; **Senior:** £7.00; **Child:** £6.00.

Blackpool Standard 159 has been a stalwart of the museum's tramway since it opened in 1972. **Shaun Courtnage**

Fleet details:			
No.	**Origin**	**Built**	**Status**
11	Blackpool	1939	Operational
14	Lowestoft	1904	Under restoration
159	Blackpool	1927	Operational
474	Amsterdam	1929	Stored
488	Glasgow	1901	Under restoration. Ffestiniog Railway
513	Sheffield	1950	Operational. On loan from Beamish
1858	London	1930	Operational

Black Country Living Museum
Dudley

Vital Statistics

Established: 1979
Owned and Operated by: Black Country Living Museum Trust
Route mileage: Approximately 0.35 (0.6km)
Power supply: 550V DC overhead line
Gauge: 4ft 8½in (1435mm)
Address: Tipton Road, Dudley, DY1 4SQ
Website: www.bclm.co.uk

The Route

From the museum entrance the tramway is a single track route throughout its length. Trams take a right hand curve to a straight section of line that crosses the trolleybus route at a near right angle. The line then bears left alongside the road and terminates close to the recreated town and alongside the two road tram depot.

Opening Times

The museum is open Wednesday to Sunday for most of the year from 10.00 to 16.00 and daily from 27th March to 5th November from 10.00 to 17.00, check website for details.

Admission Prices

Adult: £17.50; **Concessions:** £14.00;
Child: £8.75.

Family: 2+3 £51.45; 2+2 £44.10; 1+3 £36.75.

All admission tickets are valid for a full year from the date of issue.

The Black Country Museum offers the chance to ride not only electric tramcars but trolleybuses as well. Wolverhampton & District 34 is seen outside the tram depot with Wolverhampton trolleybus 433 behind. **Mike Rhodes**

Developments

The tramway has not operated since July 2016. Official information states: Please note, our tram is undergoing essential maintenance and as such, is currently out of service. Several of our heritage vehicles will be operating a regular transport service around the site in its place.

The Museum has made a formal bid to the Heritage lottery fund for a re-development of the Museum which will include an extension of the tramway.

No.	Origin	Built	Status
5	Dudley, Stourbridge & District	1920	Under restoration. Llangollen Railway
19	Wolverhampton & District	1902	Stored, awaiting restoration
23	Wolverhampton	1892	Stored, awaiting restoration
34	Wolverhampton & District	1919	Operational
49	Wolverhampton	1909	Operational
75	Dudley, Stourbridge & District	1919	Stored, awaiting restoration
361	Lisbon	1906	Stored

Fleet details:

Museum of Scottish Industrial Life
Summerlee

Vital Statistics

Established: 1988
Owned by: North Lanarkshire Council
Operated by: Summerlee Transport Group
Route mileage: Approximately 0.25 (0.4km)
Power supply: 550V DC overhead line
Gauge: 4ft 8½in (1435mm)
Address: Heritage Way, Coatbridge, ML5 1QD
Website: www.culturenl.co.uk/summerlee/

TOWN

Depot

ENTRANCE

The Route

Starting from the museum entrance, the tramway takes a gentle right hand curve and crosses Gartsherrie Burn over a stone bridge before arriving at the two road depot. Trams turn sharply right and continue to the terminus adjacent to the miners' cottages. The route is single track throughout.

Opening Times

The museum is open daily, all year round except 25th/26th December and 1st/2nd January, from 10.00 to 17.00 (until 16.00 November – March).

Admission Prices

Admission to the museum is free.

A day ticket for tram rides costs £1.00 and is available from the museum shop.

Lanarkshire Tramway Company no.53, built in 1908, is one of the star attractions at Summerlee. The well kept tram is part of the operational fleet. 23rd October 2016.
Christopher Yapp

Fleet details:			
No.	**Origin**	**Built**	**Status**
53	Lanarkshire	1908	Operational
392	Dusseldorf	1950	Operational
1017	Glasgow	1904	Operational
1245	Glasgow	1939	Undergoing restoration

Wirral Heritage Tramway
Birkenhead

Vital Statistics

Established: 1995
Owned by: Wirral Council
Operated by: Merseyside Tramway Preservation Society
Route mileage: Approximately 0.5 (0.8km)
Power supply: 550V DC overhead line
Gauge: 4ft 8½in (1435mm)
Address: 1 Taylor Street, Birkenhead, CH41 1BG
Website: www.mtps.co.uk

TAYLOR STREET DEPOT & MUSEUM

Pacific Road

WOODSIDE FERRY

The Route

The museum and two road depot are located at Taylor Street, at the far end of the tramway. Trams load opposite the depot then depart on a single track tramway, turning right along a short reservation leading to a right angle crossing with Canning Street, which is protected by traffic signals. The route continues around a reverse curve and a sharp right turn past Egerton Bridge, to run along a straight section at the side of the Wirral Metropolitan College. Trams then run alongside Shore Road to Pacific Road, where there is a passing loop (unusually operated with right hand running), and past the site of the former depot, which is still connected to the line. Trams continue to follow Shore Road and then briefly join it before a sharp left curve takes them down to the Woodside Ferry terminus, which features a double track terminal stub.

No.69, carrying a livery for Birkenhead Corporation Tramways, was in fact built in Hong Kong in 1992. The tram was used in Blackpool before moving to its home in Birkenhead. **Alan Robson**

National Transport Museum
Howth, Ireland

Vital Statistics

Established: 1971
Operated by: Transport Museum Society of Ireland
Address: Heritage Depot, Howth Demesne, Howth, Dublin 13
Telephone: 01 832 0427
Email: info@nationaltransportmuseum.org
Website: www.nationaltransportmuseum.org

Background

Located approximately eight miles north east of Dublin, the volunteer-run National Transport Museum of Ireland is the custodian of a number of tramcars of Irish heritage. Included in the collection is an ex-London trailer restored to represent a former Dublin trailer in its latter day electrified condition.

Opening Times

The museum is open on Saturdays, Sundays and Bank Holidays from 14.00 until 17.00, check website for details.

Admission Prices

Adult: €3.00; **Senior:** €1.25; Child: €1.25; **Family:** €8.00.

Fleet details:

No.	Origin	Built	Status
N/a	Dublin United (Director's car)	1901	Static display
9	Giant's Causeway	1889	Static display
9	Hill of Howth	1902	Static display
253	Dublin United	1928	Static display
284	Dublin United	1928	Static display
T124	London County Council (trailer)	1915	Static display – fictitiously as Dublin 224

Streetlife Museum of Transport
Hull

Vital Statistics
Established: 1989
Operated by: Hull Museums
Address: Museums Quarter, High Street, Hull, HU1 1PS
Telephone: 01482 613902
Email: info@hullcc.gov.uk
Website: www.hullcc.gov.uk*
This is the Hull Council main website address. Type the word 'Streetlife' into the search box and click your way through to the museum page.

Background
The current museum opened in 1989 and has a range of galleries which showcase the exhibits in settings relating to their past. The three trams are displayed in a recreated period street scene and include Ryde Pier car 3, dating from 1871, which is reputed to be the oldest surviving tramcar in Britain.

Opening Times
The museum is open Mondays to Saturdays from 10.00 until 17.00 and Sundays from 11.00 until 16.30.

Admission Prices
Admission is free.

Above: *Hull 132, as viewed from a mezzanine gallery.*
Below: *Ryde Pier car 3.* **James Millington x 2**

Fleet details:

No.	Origin	Built	Status
1	Portstewart	1882	Static display
3	Ryde Pier	1871	Static display
132	Hull	1909	Static display. On loan from TMS, Crich

Riverside Museum
Glasgow

Vital Statistics

Established: 2011
Operated by: Glasgow Life
Address: Riverside Museum, 100 Pointhouse Place, Glasgow, G3 8RS
Telephone: 0141 287 2720
Email: museums@glasgowlife.org.uk
Website: www.glasgowlife.org.uk/museums/riverside

Background

The Riverside Museum, located on the bank of the River Clyde in Glasgow, is the new home of the collection of the Glasgow Transport Museum, previously housed at Kelvin Hall. Established in 1962 following the closure of Glasgow's tramway system, the vehicles were originally located in the former tram workshops at Coplawhill depot in Pollokshields. The tram collection spans the history of operations in the city and includes examples of the first horse and electric trams right through to the very last tram built for, and indeed by, Glasgow Corporation, in 1952.

Opening Times

The museum is open Mondays to Thursdays and Saturdays from 10.00 until 17.00; Fridays and Sundays from 11.00 until 17.00.

Admission Prices

Admission is free.

Glasgow Cunarder 1392 is one of the centrepiece exhibits at the Riverside Museum. Built as recently as 1952, it spent only a short time in service in Glasgow. The surrounding exhibits make it hard to photograph. **Tony Caddick**

Fleet details:			
No.	**Origin**	**Built**	**Status**
543	Horse car	1894	Static display
672	Room and Kitchen single deck car	1898	Static display
779	Unvestibuled, balcony Standard	1900	Static display
1088	Enclosed Standard	1924	Static display
1089	Experimental single deck car	1926	Static display
1173	Coronation	1938	Static display
1392	Cunarder	1952	Static display

London Transport Museum
Acton Museum Depot, London

Vital Statistics

Established: 1980
Operated by: Transport for London
Location 1: London Transport Museum, Covent Garden Piazza, London, WC2E 7BB
Location 2: Acton Museum Depot, 118-120 Gunnersbury Lane, Acton Town, London, W3 9BQ
Telephone: 020 7565 6344
Email: bookings@ltmuseum.co.uk
Website: www.ltmuseum.co.uk

Background

The London Transport Museum exists to conserve the transport history of London and has been based in Covent Garden since 1980, following a move from the previous facility at Syon Park. It was extensively refurbished between 2005 and 2007, with some exhibits moving to Acton Museum Depot.

Opening Times

The museum at Covent Garden is open daily throughout the year from 10.00 (11.00 on Fridays) until 18.00. Acton Museum Depot is usually opened two weekends a year, check website for details.

Only open to the public on four days per year at the Acton depot, cars 355 and 1025 are two hidden gems from London's past tramway glory. **NM**

Admission Prices

Adult: £17.50; **Concessions:** £15.00; **Child:** Free. Tickets allow unlimited entry for 12 months.

Fleet details:			
No.	**Origin**	**Built**	**Status**
102	West Ham	1910	Static display – Covent Garden
284	London Tramways Co.	1881	Static display – Covent Garden
355	Metropolitan Electric Tramways	1931	Static display – Acton depot
1025	London Transport (ex-L.C.C.)	1908	Static display – Acton depot

Jurby Transport Museum
Isle of Man

Vital Statistics

Established: 2010
Operated by: Manx Transport Trust Limited
Address: Hangar 230, Jurby Industrial Estate, Jurby, Isle of Man, IM7 3BD
Email: jtminfo@manx.net
Website: www.jtmiom.im

Background

The museum is situated in a former aircraft hangar which is now part of Jurby Industrial Estate and features a wide ranging display of transport exhibits which demonstrate the rich history of the Isle of Man.

Opening Times

As of 15th March 2017, the website and Facebook page for this museum had not been updated and was showing the 2016 opening dates. Please check for updates before you visit. The 2016 opening times were: Tuesdays, Saturdays, Sundays and Bank Holidays from 10.00 until 16.00 from April to October, closed November until Easter.

Ramsey Pier (steam outline) locomotive and coach are seen on display inside the museum. **Richard Pryke**

Admission Prices

Admission is free.

No.	Origin	Built	Status
Fleet details:			
11	Douglas Bay Horse Tramway	1886	Static display
22	Douglas Bay Horse Tramway	1890	Static display and shop
47	Douglas Bay Horse Tramway	1911	Static display
72/73	Douglas Upper Cable Tramway	1896	Static display
N/a	Ramsey Pier (locomotive and coach)	1937	Static display

NEETT, Sunderland
(North Eastern Electrical Transport Trust)

Vital Statistics

Established: 2012
Operated by: NEETT, in partnership with the North East Land, Sea and Air Museums Trust
Address: Old Washington Road, Sunderland, Tyne & Wear, SR5 3HZ
Telephone: 0191 5190662 (during museum opening hours only)
Email: info@NELSAM.org.uk
Website: www.nelsam.org.uk

Background

The North Eastern Electrical Traction Trust is based at the premises of the North East Land, Sea and Air Museum near Sunderland. Essentially interested in all forms of electric traction, the group purchased a number of redundant trams from Blackpool in 2011 and have also taken under their wings two foreign trams which had been in the UK for many years but previously had no secure future. Following the construction of a brand new depot during 2013/14, most of the collection is housed undercover.

Progress Twin-car 674+684 is stabled inside the tram depot here. Still painted in the Metro livery, the tram is one of many Blackpool cars sold to museums, groups and private individuals in 2011/2012. **DU**

Opening Times

1st April until 31st October - Daily 10.00 - 17.00. 1st November until 31st March - Daily 10.00 until dusk.

Admission Prices

Adult: £5.00; **Senior:** £3.00; **Child:** £3.00; **Family (2+2):** £13.00.

Fleet details:

No.	Origin	Built	Status
210	Graz	1949	In store
412	Krefeld	1957	Static display
647	Blackpool	1988	Static display
674	Blackpool	1961*	Static display
684	Blackpool	1960	Static display
721	Blackpool	1935	Under restoration

* Indicates date rebuilt from an earlier car

Ulster Folk & Transport Museum
Cultra

Vital Statistics

Established: 1967
Operated by: National Museums Northern Ireland
Address: 153 Bangor Road, Holywood, BT18 0EU
Telephone: 028 9042 8428
Website: www.uftm.org.uk

Background

The Ulster Folk and Transport Museum is located on the main A2 road at Cultra, approximately seven miles east of Belfast. It consists of two sites on either side of the main road, with the transport collection housed in two halls on one side. In one is displayed the Irish Railway Collection, which includes the Portstewart steam tram engine, whilst the trams are housed in the other building alongside an impressive selection of historic road vehicles.

Opening Times

March to September: Tuesday to Sunday - 10.00 to 17.00.
October to February: Tuesday to Friday 10.00 to 16.00; Saturday and Sunday 11.00 to 16.00.

Admission Prices

Adult: £9.00; **Senior:** £7.00; **Child:** £5.50; **Family (2+3):** £25.00 (1+3) £19.00. Please note admission to the Folk and Transport Museums are charged separately, although a combined adult 'same day' ticket can be purchased for a slight premium.

Fleet details:			
No.	**Origin**	**Built**	**Status**
2	Bessbrook & Newry	1885	Static display
2	Giant's Causeway (trailer)	1883	Static display
2	Portstewart (steam tram loco)	1900	Static display
4	Hill of Howth	1901	Static display
5	Giant's Causeway (trailer)	1883	Static display
118	Belfast (horse car)	1885	Static display
249	Belfast	1905	Static display
357	Belfast	1929	Static display
381	Fintona (horse car)	1883	Static display

Cliff Lifts

Babbacombe Cliff Railway

Vital Statistics

Opened: 1926
Gauge: 5ft
Route Length: 720 feet
Lift Height: 256 feet
Gradient: 1 in 2.88
Journey Time: 2 minutes 25 seconds
Address: Babbacombe Downs Road, Torquay, TQ1 3LF
Telephone: 01803 328750
Operated by: Babbacombe Cliff Railway Community Interest Company
Website: www.babbacombecliffrailway.co.uk

One of the last traditionally built cliff lifts in the country, Babbacombe Cliff Railway was the work of the Torquay Tramway Company, which was set up in 1923 to install a lift to Oddicombe Beach (to link Torquay). At a cost of £15,648, work started in December 1924 and the lift opened in 1926, transporting passengers from the cliff top to the beach. Designed by George Croydon Marks, who by this time had considerable experience of this work, it was built by Waygood Otis. The line only worked for nine years before it was bought by Torquay Corporation for £18,000 in 1935. In 1941 the beach was sealed off for security due to the Second World War and the lift closed until 1951, when £10,000 was spent on refurbishment after ten years of disuse. 2003 saw it closed for six weeks after the safety gear stopped the lift half way and the passengers had to be rescued. The railway is still open for business and in 2009 ownership transferred to the Babbacombe Cliff Railway Community Interest Company. The cars are large for a cliff lift with a capacity of 40 passengers and are designed to have the appearance of a traditional tramcar. An interesting feature of the line is the ringing of a bell at the bottom station to advise any passengers that the lift will close in 30 and 15 minutes. This bell was rescued from a Scandinavian vessel, Talga. If you are inclined, you can have a wedding service on board one of the 'trams'!

Showing the gradient to full effect, one of the passenger cars heads downhill. **Phil Wimbush**

This Cliff lift passes over Oddicombe Beach Hill road, complete with a 9ft 9in height restriction! **Phil Wimbush**

Aberystwyth Cliff Railway

Vital Statistics

Opened: 1896
Gauge: 4ft 8.5in
Route Length: 778 feet
Lift Height: 430 feet
Gradient: 1 in 2
Journey Time: 2 minutes 20 seconds
Address: Cliff Railway House, Cliff Terrace, Aberystwyth, Ceredigion, SY23 2DN
Telephone: 01970 617642
Operated by: Constitution Hill Ltd
Website: www.aberystwythcliffrailway.co.uk

The curved bay is seen to full effect from the top of the cliff lift. **Lance Cahill**

This funicular was built to transport customers to the site of an early Victorian theme park, which consisted of arcades with a restaurant at the bottom and a Camera Obscura and park at the top. Designed by George Croydon Marks, it was operated on a water balance system until it was upgraded to electric power in 1921. At 778 feet the line is the longest electrically operated British funicular railway. An unusual feature is the deep cutting it runs through. The line is now run by the charity Constitution Hill Ltd, a group of local volunteers. In a rather novel and pleasing manner, both the carriages are named, Lord Geraint and Lord Marks. They also carry small destination boards!

East Cliff Railway
Bournemouth

Vital Statistics

Opened: 1908
Gauge: 5ft 8in
Route Length: 166 feet
Lift Height: 118 feet
Gradient: 1 in 1.5
Journey Time: 55 seconds
Address: East Overcliff Drive, Meyrick Road, Bournemouth
Telephone: 01202 451451
Operated by: Bournemouth Borough Council
Website: www.bournemouth.gov.uk*
This is the Bournemouth Council main website address. Type 'cliff lifts' into the search box.

Showing the extent of the landslide and the two carriages now touching each other! **Alwyn Ladell**

Bournemouth East Cliff Lift opened on 16th April 1908 and is the oldest of three operating lifts in Bournemouth. It was built by Waygood-Otis and Harrison & Co., and links an art gallery and museum on the East Cliff with the beach. The cars are very similar in style to those on the Fisherman's Walk Lift; they were built as recently as 2007 and carry 12 passengers. The previous cars were built in the 1960s and had an aluminium shell. The lift was electrically operated with a 25hp motor from its inception. Originally a driver was based at the top station with an assistant at the bottom station. This continued until 1987 when an electronic control system was installed.

Heavy rainfall and gale-force winds on 26th April 2016 affected the whole of the UK, with coastal areas taking a severe battering. During the night, at the peak of the storm, a landslide occurred adjacent to the East Cliff Railway. It partially submerged the tracks in debris, moved one track closer to the other and destroyed the public toilet block at the bottom. No-one was injured and fortunately the carriages were stored in the centre of the line so therefore were relatively unscathed although they ended up touching each other due to the movement of the rails! The lift remains out of use at the time of writing, with remedial work ongoing.

West Cliff Railway
Bournemouth

Vital Statistics

Opened: 1908
Gauge: 5ft 8in
Route Length: 102 feet
Lift Height: 118 feet
Gradient: 1 in 1.42
Journey Time: 40 seconds
Address: St Michaels Road, West Cliff, Bournemouth
Telephone: 01202 451451
Operated by: Bournemouth Borough Council
Website: www.bournemouth.gov.uk*
This is the Bournemouth Council main website address. Type 'cliff lifts' into the search box.

Like the East Cliff Lift, the West Cliff Lift was also built by Waygood-Otis and Harrison & Co. It also opened in 1908, although slightly later on 1st August 1908. Like all of Bournemouth's cliff lifts, the original cars were based on the town's tram cars; these were originally powered by a 25 hp electric motor, operated by a driver at the top and an assistant at the bottom. This was replaced in the 1960s by a 28 hp three phase motor. Also in the 1960s new aluminium bodied cars were built, designed to be interchangeable between all three of the town's cliff lifts. 1987 saw the full length of the track replaced and the 1990s saw the installation of an electronic control system.

*The drab brown and cream livery is often commented on and also - for less intelligent people - the arrows do not indicate the direction of travel! **Tim Plowman***

Fisherman's Walk Cliff Lift
Bournemouth

Vital Statistics

Opened: 1935
Gauge: 5ft 10in
Route Length: 128 feet
Lift Height: 91 feet
Gradient: 1 in 1.5
Journey Time: 50 seconds
Address: Southbourne Overcliff Drive, Bournemouth
Telephone: 01202 451451
Operated by: Bournemouth Borough Council
Website: www.bournemouth.gov.uk*

This is the Bournemouth Council main website address. Type 'cliff lifts' into the search box.

Built in 1935 by Bournemouth Corporation and designed by the borough engineer Mr F P Delamore, the UK's shortest cliff lift is just 128 feet long. It was designed to serve the Southbourne and Boscombe promenades and has two 12 seater passenger cars. The lift was originally powered by a 21 hp 500V DC motor which was replaced in the 1960s. It is a very simple little line with modest stations at both ends.

Close-up of the two carriages that work here. **Andrew Murray**

Bridgnorth Cliff Railway

Vital Statistics

Opened: 1892
Gauge: 3ft 8.5in
Route Length: 201 feet
Lift Height: 111 feet
Gradient: 1 in 1.81
Journey Time: 1 minute 25 seconds
Address: 6a Castle Terrace, Bridgnorth, WV16 4AH
Telephone: 01746 762052
Operated by: Bridgnorth Castle Hill Railway Company Ltd
Website: www.bridgnorthcliffrailway.co.uk

In stark comparison to the West Cliff lift at Bournemouth, the gorgeous livery carried by these carriages makes them a popular attraction. **Roger Cutler**

This line was opened on 7th July 1892 by George Croydon Marks, who unusually became the first Managing Director, closely followed by his brother Edward. The line links the Low Town of Bridgnorth with the High Town, opposite Bridgnorth Castle, and is England's only inland electric cliff railway. When first opened, it was powered by a system using water and gravity: water was pumped into a 2,000 gallon tank beneath the top car until its weight overcame the lower car. The tank was emptied once the car reached the lower station. Unusually the cliff lift was rebuilt during the war years of 1943 and 1944 and modified to use electricity, reopening on 9th May 1944. The original cars were replaced in 1955 by the distinctive aluminium monocoque ones still used today. Also in 1955 new winding gear was installed below the top station, of the same type as was formerly used in collieries. The railway is still run by the original owning company and in 2011 was in the hands of the cousins of the founder George Croydon Marks.

Leas Cliff Lift
Folkestone

Vital Statistics

Opened: 1885
Gauge: 5ft 10in
Route Length: 164 feet
Lift Height: 100 feet
Gradient: 1 in 1.192
Journey Time: 50 seconds
Address: Lower Sandgate Road, Folkestone, CT20 1QJ
Telephone: 01303 210047
Operated by: Leas Lift Community Interest Company
Website: www.visitkent.co.uk/attractions/the-leas-lift/135584

Opened on 16th September 1885, this is one of the oldest water-balance cliff lifts still running. Using the water and gravity system which is operated from a small cabin at the top of the cliff, all of the water is recycled. Due to its phenomenal success, a second was installed alongside in 1888; although now disused, those tracks can still be seen. Two more were built further along the Leas cliff, showing the area's popularity. Formerly in private ownership, the lift was taken over in 1967 by the local council. When the lease expired in 2009 it passed into the hands of The Leas Lift Community Interest Company, following the council's decision that the lift was too expensive to maintain. In 2011 significant restoration work was undertaken which included mechanical work, re-profiling the cars' tyres, replacement of steelwork in the water storage tanks, replacing the electrical wiring and overhauls of the power pumps.

It is hard to believe that back in 1888 passenger numbers were so high that a second system was built alongside! Clearly showing that now disused section, once again the restored period buildings add to the attraction. **Thomas Cogley**

West Hill Railway
Hastings

Vital Statistics

Opened: 1891
Gauge: 6ft
Route Length: 500 feet
Lift Height: 170 feet
Gradient: 1 in 2.9
Journey Time: 1 minute 40 seconds
Address: West Hill, George Street, Hastings
Telephone: 01424 451111
Operated by: Hastings Borough Council
Website: www.visit1066country.com/things-to-do/attractions/cliff-railways-p411571

The Hastings West Hill Railway, or West Hill Lift, as it is more commonly known, opened on 7th July 1892, powered by a gas engine. An unusual feature is that it runs predominantly within a tunnel for 402 feet of its 500 feet length! It offers a useful link between George Street in the Old Town to Hastings Castle and St. Clement's Caves and offers great views of Beachy Head. It was built, despite local opposition, by the line's first operator, The Hastings Lift Company. Construction costs doubled and put the line into financial difficulty. Following bankruptcy in 1894, it was taken over by The Hastings Passenger Lift Company which ran it until 1947 when it was bought by the local council. 1971 saw the line converted to electric operation. To celebrate its centenary year in 1991 a full refurbishment was carried out.

*This system has the very unusual feature of a tunnel! By its very nature this is exceptionally rare for a cliff lift. The exquisitely built brickwork of the tunnel and sides can be seen to good effect here. **David Henderson***

East Hill Railway
Hastings

Vital Statistics

Opened: 1903
Gauge: 5ft
Route Length: 267 feet
Lift Height: 261 feet
Gradient: 1 in 1.28
Journey Time: 54 seconds
Address: Rock-a-Nore Road, Hastings
Telephone: 01424 451111
Operated by: Hastings Borough Council
Website: www.visit1066country.com/things-to-do/attractions/cliff-railways-p411571

Opened in 1903 by Hastings Borough Council, this is the steepest funicular railway in Great Britain with a gradient of 1 in 1.28. It provides access to Hastings Country Park with the lower part of the line running in a rock cutting. Originally worked on the water-based principle, for which the twin towers at the top station were used as water tanks, the line was converted to run on electricity during 1973-76 and the original cars were replaced. In June 2007 the line was closed after a control panel fault caused the cars to stop incorrectly, damaging both cars and stations. A huge investment began in 2008 with new cars, control gear and associated safety systems as well as repairs to the stations, which allowed re-opening in March 2010.

The rugged cliff face and restored period buildings add to the beauty of this system. **Keith Pharo**

Lynton & Lynmouth Cliff Railway

Vital Statistics
Opened: 1890
Gauge: 3ft 9in
Route Length: 862 feet
Lift Height: 500 feet
Gradient: 1 in 1.75
Journey Time: 2 minutes 30 seconds
Address: Lee Road, Lynton, EX35 6HW
Telephone: 01598 735908
Operated by: Lynmouth & Lynton Lift Co.
Website: www.cliffrailwaylynton.co.uk

The open balconies of these cars make them very popular with holidaymakers. **Phil Wimbush**

Opened on Easter Monday in 1890 between the twin towns of Lynton and Lynmouth as a water-powered funicular railway, this is another of George Croydon Marks' designs. Unusually it has an intermediate stop below Lynton Station, which was used to transport goods. The car body could be removed to transport bulky items, including cars! The two operating cars, each with room for 40 passengers, are joined by a continuous cable running around a pulley at each end of the incline. Water is fed through a pipe from the West Lyn River and fills tanks fixed underneath the car at the top of the incline. Water is released from the lower car until the top car descends, with speed controlled by a brakeman inside each car. In recognition of its historic nature the railway is classified as a listed monument.

Scarborough Spa Cliff Lift

Vital Statistics

Opened: 1875
Gauge: 4ft 8.5in
Route Length: 286 feet
Lift Height: 84 feet
Gradient: 1 in 1.75
Journey Time: 47 seconds
Address: Scarborough Spa, South Bay,
  Scarborough, YO11 2HD
Telephone: 01723 821888
Operated by: Scarborough Spa
Website: www.scarboroughspa.co.uk/cliff_lift

*View of the top station, just off the Esplanade. **DU***

Opened by the Scarborough South Cliff Tramway Company Limited on 6th July 1875, this was the first funicular railway in the United Kingdom, built to link the South Cliff Esplanade to the Scarborough Spa. The line was built by Crossley Brothers of Manchester and the carriages were built by the Metropolitan Carriage Company of Birmingham. Initially the cars were moved by a counterweight system, with water tanks carried under each car, the water being pumped by a hydraulic system powered by gas engines. These only lasted four years and were replaced in 1879 by steam pumps, which continued in service until a major refurbishment in 1934-35 by Hudswell, Clarke & Company, traditionally a steam engine builder. (Incidentally this company also built two diesel powered steam outline locomotives for the nearby North Bay Railway in 1931 and 1932.) A new electric motor was installed and the cars were replaced, surviving to this day with little change except slight modifications to provide better access for passengers. Scarborough Borough Council purchased the lift in 1993 and made the operation completely automatic in 1997.

The simple cars offer fine views of the bay and sea. *DU*

Saltburn Cliff Lift

Vital Statistics

Opened: 1884
Gauge: 4ft 2in
Route Length: 207 feet
Lift Height: 120 feet
Gradient: 1 in 1.40
Journey Time: 55 seconds
Address: Lower Promenade, Saltburn, TS12 2QX
Telephone: 01287 622528
Operated by: Redcar and Cleveland Borough Council
Website: www.saltburnbysea.com/html/clifflift.html

Replacing a mechanical hoist which had been declared unsafe the previous year, this lift was designed and installed by George Croydon Marks, opening on 28th June 1884. It is operated by water, which flows into tanks underneath the car at the top station, so the weight takes it down the gradient and pulls the other car up. Once it reaches the bottom the tank is emptied. It was originally powered by a four-cylinder Crossley combustion engine pump, which survived until 1913 when a DC generator and pump were installed. This in turn was replaced relatively quickly when in 1924 an AC electrically operated water pump was installed, which is still in use. The operation is controlled by a brakeman who sits in a small cabin at the top. At the bottom are lavish buildings including a ticket office, waiting room and engine room, sharing a similarity with all cliff lifts - that the traffic is always busier going uphill! Following the Second World War the lift was bought by the council. Originally the cars had stained glass windows which were lost when the car bodies were replaced in 1955. The cars were replaced again in 1979 (based on the original design) and stained glass windows were installed in 1991. The braking wheel was replaced for the first time in 1998. 2014 saw a full refurbishment of the top station to original design. The Saltburn Cliff Lift is the oldest water-balanced funicular in the United Kingdom. The carriages were restored in 2010 and returned in Easter 2011, just in time for the town's 150th anniversary.

The top station operator's room. **John Carter**

The classic shot at Saltburn showing the cliff lifts and the pier. 681 feet in length, the pier was built in 1869 and pre-dates the cliff lift by 15 years. **John Carter**

Central Tramway
Scarborough

Vital Statistics

Opened: 1881
Gauge: 4ft 8.5in
Route Length: 234 feet
Lift Height: 81 feet
Gradient: 1 in 2.8
Journey Time: 38 seconds
Address: Marine Parade, Scarborough, YO11 2ER
Telephone: 01723 501754
Operated by: Central Tramway Company
Website: www.centraltramway.co.uk

Fine views of the bay and North Sea can be found at the top of this lift. The attractive traditional livery of the carriages adds to the scene. **William Wright**

The Central Tramway Company was formed in 1880 and began operations on 1st August 1881, making it the oldest tramway company still in existence. The line runs between the town centre (north side of the Grand Hotel) and the beach. Originally powered by steam, the steam house was situated away from the tramway at the top station. Drivers had no view of the cars and relied on markings on a rope to stop the cars in the correct unloading place. 1910 saw the power supply changed to electricity and in 1932 the motor was placed under the top station, meaning the cars could now be driven from there. The cars were also replaced in the same year. In 1975 a fire damaged the carriages, with replacements purchased from George Neville Truck Equipment of Kirkby in Ashfield. In 2009 an automated drive system was installed along with new motors. Three years later significant restoration of the buildings and carriages took place, making this a superb example of a working cliff lift.